BREAKTHROUGH TENNIS

A Revolutionary Approach to the Game

ROLF CLARK

Farragut Publishing Company
Washington, D.C.

PRINTED IN THE UNITED STATES OF AMERICA

Cover photograph by Terje Rakkae/THE IMAGE BANK
Cover and text design by Jann Alexander Design
Typography by Chronicle Type & Design

Library of Congress Cataloging-in-Publication Data
Clark, Rolf, 1937-
    Breakthrough tennis: a revolutionary approach to the game / by Rolf
Clark
        p. cm.
    Includes index
    ISBN 0-918535-11-5: $9.95
    1. Tennis—Psychological aspects.   2. Tennis.   I. Title.
GV1002.9.P75C57 1991
798.342'01—dc20   91-3070
                                                                              CIP

To Kelly and Robert

Acknowledgments

Gary Lester and Herb Tanzer planted the seeds for this book with their seminar, The Forum—a philosophical inquiry into the way we think, act and communicate.

Friends and students on the tennis court have helped sharpen the thoughts behind *Breakthrough Tennis*. I single out Jane Marden, a friend and tennis associate, who insisted these thoughts be expressed, encouraged me to persist, and suggested improvements throughout. Arnold Rosenberg served as a verbal backboard. Marilyn Herman tried these concepts on the court and then suggested ways to express them better. Best-selling author Jean Carper gently but firmly tried to show me how to write for people instead of academicians. Lisa Berger advised me on the publication process.

Dan Rapoport spent valuable time asking for corrections, editing and revising the results, and (I think) secretly testing the ideas on the court. His publishing this book must mean they worked for him.

Rolf Clark

The Publisher's Response

Author Rolf Clark suspects correctly. During the editing of *Breakthrough Tennis,* I did indeed test its ideas on the court. And yes, my publishing his manuscript means they do work.

But I publish with some reluctance. My tennis partners, especially those who battled me evenly over the years, have accused me of holding up publication in order to achieve and maintain an edge over them. Maybe so. I guess it's only fair that I share Rolf's secrets with the world—and my opponents.

You who are about to read *Breakthrough Tennis* and apply it to your game are in store for a remarkable experience. You are going to play tennis better than you've ever imagined and enjoy it more than ever before.

Daniel Rapoport

CONTENTS

PROLOGUE

The Origins of
Breakthrough Tennis

I took up tennis as a sport 13 years ago, when I turned 41. I loved the game, learned to play and practiced hard. Yet seven years later, after taking 50 or more lessons and reading numerous books, I was dismayed. My game was not what it should have been. I'd lose to people I should have beaten.

Moreover, I was getting tennis elbow. That was the kicker.

I'm a college professor. I teach engineering students about systems and systems thinking, a way to find the crucial factors that control complex processes. Applying systems thinking to the complex process of hitting tennis balls led me to think first about the principles of physics that affect the swing—particularly momentum and the laws of motion.

I experimented with the timing of my strokes by swinging my racket at different speeds, using different body motions. I was trying to find what timing put the least pressure on my elbow. Given my background, it seemed natural to consider Newton's Law of Action and Reaction—something I knew had to be at the core of the backswing/forward swing sequence. Allowing the forward swing to be a natural reaction to the backswing—the essence of Newton—improved my timing dramatically.

I also started to think about balance. I noticed that my balance on the court was inconsistent, and I experimented with that. The physics of weight transfer affect balance, and being balanced made it easier to improve the timing of my swing.

Almost concurrently I began to analyze the way I was approaching the game mentally. I would try to recall what was on my mind as I played—what I was concentrating on when I played well, what I was concentrating on when I played poorly, and what really made a difference in terms of results.

Through my years as a student and teacher I had come to realize that true learning evolves from inquiry by the student, not from explanation or answers provided by a teacher or others. It was this kind of process that I was going through with my tennis game. I observed the way I played. I thought about the physics principles that are fundamental to tennis. I examined my mental game.

I began playing differently. I began playing better. The change was startling. "Breakthrough" was the only way I could describe the transformation that was taking place in my game.

Before my breakthrough I was a frustrated club player. Within two years, which included further breakthroughs, I was a ranked senior in my region, competing against ex-college players and men who had played in the Davis Cup and even at Wimbledon. Most important, my philosophy toward tennis had changed. The game was now a source of genuine, constant and lasting enjoyment. In looking back on my experience I arrived at several conclusions.

Like most players, I had realized for a long time that the mental side of tennis was important. However, my breakthrough showed me that I had been woefully underestimating how important.

After years of learning tennis the traditional way, I discovered that simply trying to do what a tennis instructor says does not really work. If you're a serious student of the game, you have to become actively involved in exploring your own tennis.

And what you explore is crucial. Concentrating on the usual mechanics—turning sideways, getting your racket back early, stepping forward, following through—leads to unnatural tennis. The thinking you expend on those mechanics distracts your mind from the single most important act of tennis: hitting the ball.

Your success in hitting the ball will depend on whether you correctly apply such principles of physics as momentum and the Laws of Motion. Don't worry, although many of the concepts in *Breakthrough Tennis* are based on physics, you needn't know anything about the subject in order to develop your game. My brief discussion of physics is non-technical and easily understood by laymen. In fact, thinking about these principles—instead of mechanics—will help you focus on the few essentials you must understand to control your game.

The real fundamentals of tennis, the mastery of which leads to natural tennis, are *concentration, timing* and *balance*:

- *Concentration* is what you do with your mind and eyes, and it's employed differently in practice and competition.
- *Timing* refers to when and how you swing your racket.
- *Balance* means your equilibrium and body control, whether you are standing or in motion. Balance affects your power, quickness and timing.

These fundamentals cannot be explained to you. You need to be *aware* of them yourself. You need to feel your physical game and observe your mental game. Then you'll start to understand what works for you and what doesn't.

A teaching pro can be part of the breakthrough tennis experience; he or she can help you explore both the physical and mental games. But real improvement requires that you become the one who learns tennis, rather than one who is taught tennis.

Who This Book Is For

Breakthrough Tennis is for players who are unsatisfied with their progress, for players who feel they have peaked at a plateau that is below their potential. That's most of us. It is also for instructors trying to help us.

While not specifically written for beginners, *Breakthrough Tennis* will keep them from learning the game the wrong way. Advanced players who have stalled at an unacceptable level of play can find suggestions, especially for the mental game, that will get them back on an upward track.

But, most of all, *Breakthrough Tennis* is for the frustrated intermediate—the player who would like to be better, who feels he or she has the capability to be better, who has taken numerous lessons and who might even aspire to becoming an advanced player. Included in this category is the player resigned to the false notion that age or lack of coordination precludes hope for improvement.

If those learning or improving can benefit from *Breakthrough Tennis*, then so can instructors. At first blush this may sound strange; I differ with much of today's conventional teaching of tennis. But since this book is about new ways to approach learning the game, it should be of interest to those teaching it. I have discussed *Breakthrough Tennis* with numerous instructors, and they have reacted enthusiastically. I hope other instructors will be open to these ideas, and experiment with the principles in their own teaching. *Breakthrough Tennis* calls upon pupil and teacher to explore together what works and what doesn't work for each pupil.

If you're like most readers, you live a busy life with a limited amount of time to spend on tennis. You want to play tennis well but don't expect to become a professional. You will practice, so long as practice is recreational. Working at practice is acceptable; suffering isn't. *Breakthrough Tennis* has been written for people like you, for tennis players who live in the real world.

I want to note here that my approach owes a debt to W. Timothy Gallwey and his classic work *The Inner Game of Tennis* (Random House, 1974). He presented a way to learn through "letting" tennis happen. His Zen-like tennis called for allowing the body, with its subconscious computational skills, to do what it does remarkably well: operate without continual advice from the conscious mind.

Still, many of us are unable to develop the mental state Gallwey's Inner Game requires. It demands a form of concentration based on Eastern philosophies largely foreign to the Western mind. We Westerners want to understand subjects quickly, and if improvement is possible, we believe that it will take place more rapidly if we make it happen rather than allow it to happen. Thus we want to know causes and effects.

Breakthrough Tennis deals with the causes and effects of tennis play. It offers the reader many new insights into both the physical *and* mental games. It identifies specifics that can be explored—without the burdensome details that Gallwey and I abhor.

What Breakthroughs Are Like

Jean had taken lessons for ten years and felt she was getting nowhere. Her first breakthrough occurred in a thirty-minute session at the local club. It happened not on the court but in front of mirrors at an aerobics center. We started talking Newton and timing. I asked her to experiment with swinging the racket and to watch herself in the mirrors. I was hoping for a well-timed swing in which her arm and racket virtually swung themselves.

When I thought she had her timing about right we went on the court. I asked her to keep swinging the way she had in front of the mirrors and to simply get into a position relative to the ball so she could swing that way. She *immediately* began hitting deep shots with power and grace. I hadn't told her anything about what to do, only to swing the racket the most natural way it could be swung, and to swing that way while hitting a ball.

Jean didn't necessarily understand the physics of timing but after swinging the racket smoothly for a few minutes she knew what timing felt like. Her virtually non-existent backhand became reasonably powerful, simply because she tried to swing it "like a pendulum." After the first 30 minutes she commented several times that she could not understand why it had all been so difficult before. Her description of the experience was summed up in a one-word message to a friend—"incredible."

Shortly afterward she won a set from a longtime court nemesis, something she had never come close to doing in some 25 matches.

What Jean achieved—a true breakthrough in her play—is something that you too can achieve. And like her, you can experience subsequent breakthroughs.

Once you develop the three basic playing skills of tennis—balance, timing and concentration—breakthroughs will become commonplace. You will move faster, hit more powerfully, function more efficiently and exercise greater control.

Your body will be in the right place at the right time to hit each ball and your swing will be smooth and efficient. You'll know what works for you to hit the ball well; your concentration will focus on it. A breakthrough is not a marginal change in your ability, it is a quantum leap.

You will also play more safely. You'll stress your joints and muscles less as your movement becomes more graceful and efficient. As a consequence, your tennis life will be extended.

These breakthroughs will occur no matter your age, experience, condition, or playing ability.

Now, I don't want to suggest that you will always play well or stroke perfectly. Yes, break*downs* too will occur, times when nothing you do will seem to work. Yet you will find that those slumps will become fewer, last a shorter period of time and will be easier to correct than previous ones. You're also likely to find that, even when you lose a match, you rarely will unravel.

The point to keep in mind is that breakthroughs can occur weekly, and sometimes even happen in a working span of five or ten minutes.

PART ONE

HOW WE LEARN

BREAKTHROUGH TENNIS WORKS NOT ONLY BE-cause of what it says about how to play tennis but also about how to learn tennis. Its "revolutionary approach to the game" enlists the student to serve as his own teacher. An instructor can be of help, but you will achieve a breakthrough only if you, the one person who knows the student better than anyone else, shape your newfound knowledge to your special requirements.

Before you can learn, you must know *how* to learn.

1

Exploration:
The Learning Tool

IN ORDER TO LEARN WHAT IS NECESSARY TO SCORE A BREAK-through in your tennis game you will have to "explore" your play. This exploration will be a never ending process—with never ending rewards.

Exploration, in the sense that I use it, means inquiry into the action you are trying to master. When the inquiry is carried out consciously it resembles experimenting. When it's done subconsciously, it takes the form of trial and error. In either case, we end up practicing what works. What feels right. We learn lots of difficult things that way.

For example, when it came time to teach my daughter to ride a two-wheeler, I told her what to do with her hands, where to put her feet, and what to do with her knees. But listening to what I told her didn't help her. She learned how to ride by exploring balance. She got on the bike and struggled with balance until, through trial and error, she got it.

We learn to walk by trial and error—getting up, falling down, getting up—until we stay up. Our parents couldn't explain walking to us. We saw others walk, and walking became a possibility. Without realizing it, we explored the possibility. We didn't copy the mechanics of anyone's walk; we walked our way.

Exploration, not description, helped us walk and ride bikes. Tennis is much the same. You explore something in your tennis game by observing how you do it—by becoming aware of what you do—and then doing it in different ways until it feels right. Exploring requires mental awareness of physical sensations. Your mind observes and your body senses. If the sensations are not perfect, you keep experimenting.

Learn to Learn for Yourself

Many of us learn tennis by taking lessons. The lessons help for a while, and when things go wrong again we take another lesson. We come to rely on the instructor to tell us what's wrong without being actively engaged in that question ourselves. Between lessons, when the instructor is not guiding us, our tennis goes downhill. It shouldn't be that way. We should be able to improve all the time, without continual assistance.

There are things the instructor really can't teach us. Like balance. You need to *feel* balance. And while instructors can coach you on timing, they cannot explain it. You need to sense it yourself.

Keep in mind that tennis professionals are naturals. They don't have trouble with their timing or their balance. Learning about balance and timing from someone who never had trouble with either is like learning about water from a fish. The fish doesn't know there is such a thing as water. To help you, an instructor needs your help. You need to let the instructor know how things feel. As you express yourself, you and the instructor become more aware of things to explore.

Explore tennis on your own. Explore it through lessons too. But learn to be involved in the lessons. Don't ask the instructor to be responsible for your learning.

Don't be a sponge, only absorbing. Let the pro know what seems to make sense and what doesn't, how you need time to work on this or that before trying something else. Good pros will want this kind of information. They'll try to coach you in what you want to learn, not force-feed you what they think you should try.

Awareness Is Part of It

In our culture, we count on succeeding through analysis, explanation, and action. We are oriented toward establishing goals and attaining them on time, by focusing our effort on the process that leads to the goals. This works well when the task is well-defined, like assembling a cabinet or filling out your income tax forms.

It doesn't work at all well when the process being explored is not well-defined. Like walking or riding a bike. Or tennis.

Tennis lends itself to exploration. It's better to be aware of your tennis as it is and to allow it to change, rather than to try to fix it through analysis and explanation. A good pro will help you learn about your tennis and how it feels, then give you coaching in what to explore. But too many pros try to fix your tennis for you.

We Need to
Rethink the Way We Think

Normally we see a problem and want the answer.

That doesn't work in tennis.

The reason answers aren't the answer is that once you have an answer you stop inquiring into the process you're working on.

If you believe that "bring the racket back early" cures your problem of hitting late—and it may well cure it temporarily— then you stop exploring the feeling of lateness in your swing, and you never get to the real source of your problem. The true cause of the problem could be your failure to react or your failure to concentrate on the impact point. Or it could be that you are too close to the ball or are making other basic errors that disrupt your game.

There are things that will make a difference in your tennis if *you* think of them—things that are specific to you or the way you move and concentrate, things that you may not have thought of thinking about.

I don't know the dimensions that will cause breakthroughs for you. Only you can find them for sure. But I can give you examples from my experience.

Why So Few Pictures ?

You can't take pictures of the important things.

We love pictures. They're "worth a thousand words." But not in tennis. This book has very few pictures showing how to swing. There's a good reason.

You can only take pictures of the mechanical parts of tennis. Photographs of feet and shoulders and grips. Of bent knees and ready positions.

A sequence of pictures can show shoulder turns and follow-throughs and footwork. Or forehand and backhand sequences.

Those are useful but there's no way to photograph the essential things. Like balance. Like timing. Or how to react to the ball. Or how to concentrate. Or how to anticipate.

These are the guts of tennis. Looking at too many picture sequences in a book on tennis reinforces the impression that tennis is a set of mechanics.

It isn't. To really learn tennis you need to explore it in your mind. Your mind can explore areas that cameras can't.

Not until I explored what distracted me from hitting well consistently did I find that my mind was not on hitting the ball but on where I wanted to hit. That's when I started to understand that "watch the ball" was not helping. My eyes could be on the ball while my *mind* was on the thought of putting the ball in the open court, which of course distracted me from hitting properly.

Not until I explored what it would feel like to hit a perfect shot did I ask questions about timing, and what that would feel like in my swing. That got me out of the charted waters of forehand and backhand technique, and into the new waters of timing. Timing didn't seem at all like what I'd spent several years trying to learn.

Not until I thought about why men older and heavier than I could reach balls that I couldn't did it occur to me that there was a dimension called "reacting to the ball" that made an incredible difference. Focusing on reacting made me react more quickly. Sure, I'd heard of reacting but no one had told me it could produce such a payoff when it was intentionally explored.

In my explorations there were no answers, just more questions. But the questioning helped me improve in a very basic sense. I wasn't just treating symptoms; I was getting to the root causes of my problems.

I can't chart a specific path for you to explore. It will be different for each reader. But I can give you some important new dimensions to explore. They build on my experiences and those of others. Their value will be in pushing you to think in a different way about your tennis. Build on what I suggest. Tailor my suggestions to your own needs. But don't expect me, a tennis instructor or anyone else to improve your game. That's your job.

2

Stop Learning the Wrong Way

WE LEARN TENNIS INCORRECTLY. WE TRY TO DO WHAT SOME-
one else tells us to do. Someone who doesn't feel what we
feel.

At the beginning we are told: "Turn sideways to the net."
"Get your racket back early." "Keep your eye on the ball."
"Follow through." And so on.

Eventually we are inundated with these and other tennis
rules and tips. We strive to follow all of them. Often they don't
help; frequently they are harmful.

On our own we watch the pros play and try to imitate them.
That doesn't work either. It doesn't get to what's missing in our
own games.

Watching and listening do not deal with the three components of tennis that are part of every good tennis player's game:
balance, timing and concentration. You need to explore your
balance, timing and concentration. They can't be explained or
seen.

Why Rules and Tips
Don't Work

Almost everyone will tell you to "watch the ball" or "look at the ball" or "keep your eye on the ball." That's the apparent cardinal rule of the game. But watching the ball isn't the answer.

I tried watching the ball for years before I realized that trying to "watch the ball" distracted me from doing what I really needed to do, which was to *hit* the ball. A spectator in the stands can watch the ball. You can watch the ball all you want, but it's not going over the net unless your racket hits it. Of course, watching it helps you hit it. But hitting it requires more than just looking at it with your eyes. It requires something from your mind and your body. You need to keep your eyes on the ball, and your mind on hitting the ball. You need to feel your racket so you can make it meet the ball that you're watching.

Take another well-known rule: "Bring the racket back early." That's supposed to help you have time to hit. But bringing the racket back early can mess up your timing. It puts a delay in your swing. Learn about good timing and you'll bring your racket back at the right moment. More accurately, you'll start your swing at the right time, which is different. "Bring the racket back" is misleading. It causes a disconnect between your racket and your body. When you prepare to hit, you should focus on how your racket will hit the ball, not on bringing the racket back.

Even more fundamentally, we try tennis tips hoping they'll produce a good swing. It's the other way around. Swing correctly and certain results happen; then we label the results as tips. For example, consider the tip "keep a firm wrist." Keeping a firm wrist won't make you swing properly. It's swinging properly that causes your wrist to stay firm. We see that the pro doesn't use his wrist when he swings and mistakenly think the firm wrist is causing his good swing when it's really the other way around.

Many standard tennis rules and tips are simply bad advice. Turning sideways to the net, for example, can rob you of power and quickness. Most touring pros do not turn sideways to hit. Watch the power and speed of Andre Agassi. He hits facing the net more than the side of the court.

Bringing the racket too far back can disrupt your timing. Pointing at the ball to hit an overhead can throw you off balance. Trying to hit to the open court will cause you to focus on a result instead of an action—an action like meeting the ball with the racket.

Causes and results are often confused in tennis tips. Swinging with proper balance and timing will cause you to follow through completely. A complete follow-through will not cause good timing or balance.

Avoid any tip that takes your attention away from the impact itself. "Bring the racket back early" and "follow through" both put your mind on the racket, not the impact.

So what you work on is important. Most mechanical steps you try—those actions that can be described and imitated— will not make a difference in your game. And what helps one person doesn't necessarily work for someone else. No single answer exists.

In the physical game, our balance and timing can make an enormous difference, yet we usually don't work on either. No one tells us to pay attention to them, so consequently we don't think of them—if we think of them at all—as particularly important to our tennis.

In the mental game, we are instructed to "concentrate" and told how crucial concentration is to effective tennis. But we're rarely told what concentration is or how to improve it. Exploring concentration and experiencing good concentration will produce huge payoffs.

Be Wary of Imitating the Pros

Copying the experts fails for at least two reasons. One, few of us have their natural athletic abilities. What they can do easily is not necessarily easy for us. Trying to hit like someone who is a much better athlete than you are will be frustrating.

The second reason why imitating the pros doesn't work is that they play differently from each other. Whom would you imitate? Michael Chang hits his two-handed backhand with topspin, Jimmy Connors hits his flat and hard, and Martina Navratilova uses controlled underspin on her one-hander. Some advanced players hit their forehands off their right foot, some off their left, and many hit off either one depending on the circumstances.

McEnroe plays volleys with graceful touch, Becker hits his with driving power. If there were one best way to hit, the pros

---

Tennis Tips Don't Work

Work on what's right and you'll discard the 100 tennis tips you've heard. Most of them are wrong or at least misleading. Here are a few popular ones to ignore.

"Bring the racket back early" violates a law of physics, that of action and reaction. Bring the racket back too early, and you're forced to hold it behind you, waiting for the ball. That disrupts the natural timing of your swing.

"Hold the racket firmly at impact" is unnecessary advice unless your timing and balance are off. If that's the case you're going to be holding it firmly in order to muscle the racket through the ball to compensate for your lack of rhythm. Swing with good timing, and you can hold the racket like you'd hold a small bird.

"Get to the ball early" can make you hit off-balance, especially if you tend to overrun the ball. You should get to the ball at just the right time—not early, not late—so that your swing can flow freely when you hit.

"Concentrate!" is an exhortation, an incomplete tip, that we frequently demand of ourselves. It's not useful. Concentrate on what? And when?

---

would all hit that way. Imitating the actions of different players leads to playing with a hodgepodge of copied techniques, some of which only the super-athlete can execute. The effort you put into imitation is likely to lead only to a disruption of your own timing and balance.

To play naturally you need to develop your own skills. Once you come to understand your way of playing, try to find a teaching pro who hits more or less like you do and use him or her to refine your own technique. Note the irony. I'm telling you that in order to hit better, find a pro who hits like you do. That's different from trying to copy a pro.

3

Now Let's Learn the Right Way

YOUR GOAL IN DEVELOPING A SOLID TENNIS GAME IS NOT simply to play well. It's to play *naturally*. You want to learn to position yourself and swing in a way that is natural to *you*. This doesn't mean, however, that there aren't some things in tennis that we all must learn pretty much the same way.

Although tennis pros and other fine players each have their own styles, they all come close to mastering the three underlying components of the game: balance, timing and concentration.

No matter what their individual techniques, all tennis pros are balanced during and between hits.

They time their swings to meet the ball smoothly and powerfully.

They focus their attention on the actions that affect the way the ball is hit, meaning they concentrate well.

Pay attention to your balance, timing and concentration. They affect everyone's game—Bjorn Borg's, Steffi Graf's, yours and mine.

They are at the heart of *Breakthrough Tennis*.

Balance enables you to move about the court efficiently. It is also a prerequisite for proper timing.

Timing determines the power and consistency of your strokes. It's about the way you swing to hit the ball.

Concentration is what your eyes and mind pay attention to as you play. Pay attention to the right things and you're likely to play well; concentrate on the wrong things and your game suffers.

Balance, timing and concentration are not what we usually work on when we practice. Instead, we try to master those tennis tips like "step into the ball," "keep a firm wrist" or "follow through."

But tips make you mechanical. You wind up playing tennis the way you would walk if you thought about the mechanics of walking: Lift your left foot three inches, bend the left knee 30 degrees, stretch your leg forward and set the foot down thirteen inches from where it was, and so on.

Just as walking cannot be learned that way, neither can tennis. You need to feel tennis, not manage it.

Luckily, we've used balance, timing, and concentration all our lives. We've used them to jump puddles, shoot baskets, climb stairs, run for the bus and dance. They are already natural to us. We don't need to learn them from scratch. We simply need to let them influence our tennis more.

How do you do that? By being *aware* of them and by *exploring* them as you practice.

How Jane Learned to Hit Overheads

Jane had played tennis for five years, yet still dreaded overheads. She'd tried pointing at the ball with her left hand, turning her shoulders, bringing the racket to the backscratch position and keeping her left hip toward the net, as well as other tips she had picked up over the years. Numerous lessons had failed to help.

I asked her to forget everything she knew about hitting overheads, and simply explore her balance as she hit a few lobs with her overhead. She said she didn't know what I meant.

"Be aware of your balance, explore it, experiment with it," I told her. "Get so you *feel* balanced throughout the hit."

I told her how I explored my own balance. I said that for me it meant experimenting with my weight distribution, with the way I held my arms as I waited, and with the way I held the racket. It felt best when my weight was between my feet, both arms up over my shoulders and the racket held gently and pointing upward. I felt balanced as I waited to hit.

On the other hand, pointing at the ball with my left hand and holding my racket in the backscratch position (two well-known tips) did not seem like being balanced for me. The left hand up and the racket behind me made me feel *off* balance.

I demonstrated what I meant by being balanced as I prepared to hit an imaginary lob. I bounced lightly on my feet.

That was balance before the hit. As I hit, I felt balanced if I moved up into the ball by swinging the racket upward and launching my body fully up toward the ball with a strong leg drive. I tried to stay balanced during the upward drive.

As I completed my hit, I made sure my weight returned to the court still in balance. I was ready to move for the next shot.

It didn't seem to matter what my feet were doing. I didn't worry about "proper footwork." The footwork took care of itself if I paid attention to being balanced.

I asked her to hit me a few lobs, and demonstrated several times. I was surprised, by the way, at how effortless my overheads became as I made sure I was balanced as I hit.

Then I hit a few short lobs to Jane.

After her first three or four attempts, I could see it wasn't working as I'd hoped. I asked what she was thinking, and she replied she was trying to do what I said. I asked her not to try to do what I said—that worked for me but she would need to discover *her* balance for herself. What I'd said about how I explored balance had only been to start her thinking in the right direction. She'd have to work it out herself.

I don't know what she thought after that. It doesn't matter. Within five minutes she was hitting great overheads. Soon she was beaming with pride.

I asked her what she had done differently. She said she didn't know, she just tried to be balanced.

"Keeping my arms and racket balanced over my head seemed to make sense, so did being balanced as I landed," she went on. "It seemed to work for me to be relaxed as I hit."

Relaxation was important to her success, but I had not mentioned it. Jane had discovered it on her own through the exploration of her balance. (Someone else with whom I worked on overheads said what helped him was simply relaxing and reminding himself to be *aware* of balance as he looked up at the lob and got ready to hit it.)

Jane began exploring balance on all her strokes, with good results. She had been hitting her two-handed backhand late; now she was hitting it well out in front. She still couldn't explain what she was doing differently.

Nor should she. Awareness and exploration produce the results, explanation doesn't.

PART TWO

THE MENTAL GAME: THE MOST IMPORTANT ONE

TENNIS IS SAID TO BE 90 PERCENT MENTAL. When two people play, you can see how their physical games stack up, but you'll find it difficult to see their mental games. You can't see "concentration." Yet concentration wins. If you want to play tennis well, learn to concentrate well.

You learn concentration the same way you learn timing and balance, by exploring it—by knowing what good concentration is, by becoming aware of how *you* concentrate, by experimenting with the way you concentrate to get better results.

Concentration Wins

ERNIE IS ONE OF THE BEST PLAYERS I KNOW. HE IS IN HIS LATE forties, plays only once or twice a week and never in the winter. Yet he beats most of the young professionals in his area.

His secret is that he concentrates well. He seldom misses a makeable shot. He never loses a match he should win. But once, when he did miss a forehand, I heard him mutter, "Hit the ball, not the court!" That remark told me a lot.

When he hits the ball, he concentrates on *hitting* the ball, not on where the ball should go, not on winning the point, not on anything else taking place on the court other than his racket meeting the ball. Hitting the ball is an action. Where it should go and how the point should end are results. He concentrates on actions, not on results.

Furthermore, he said "Hit the ball," not "Watch the ball." There's a subtle difference. To hit the ball you need to watch the ball *and* make your racket meet it. The action to concentrate on is making the racket hit the ball. Watching the ball is passive—hitting it is active.

Finally, in muttering, "Hit the ball, not the court," Ernie revealed that he was *aware* of what he had been thinking, aware of what he had and had not been concentrating on when he missed his forehand. He knew, after he missed, that he'd been concentrating on the wrong objective. Instead of focusing on just hitting the ball, his mind had drifted off into thinking about where on the court he wanted to put the ball. Being aware of how you concentrate is the first step toward better concentration.

Ernie also possesses the right philosophy about tennis. If he loses but plays well, that's fine. If he wins a match but plays badly, it isn't. He is committed to playing well. To hitting each ball well. He isn't hung up on winning or losing.

I'm convinced that has a lot to do with his success.

What Exactly Is Concentration?

Perhaps the best way to define concentration is to say what it isn't. Concentration is not the same thing as "looking at" or "watching." What we look at is not always what we are concentrating on. Our minds may be on something other than what we are visually focusing on.

As I walk down the sidewalk I *watch* what is ahead of me but my mind can be concerned with the office meeting scheduled for that morning. Playing tennis that way is just not going to work.

If I am *watching* the ball but my mind is on the open court I want to hit to, I am not concentrating well. My mind should be on the same thing I am watching, namely the ball. When hitting, I should watch the ball *and* focus my mind on the racket meeting it. Nothing else.

"Focusing the mind" does not mean "thinking about." You should not be *thinking* when you play, even if you're thinking about your tennis game. You should be paying attention to what you're *doing*. Thinking about the *way* you play is something you do off the court or while exploring your game during practice.

It may be helpful to explore these mental activities and the words describing them further. When you compete, your mind should focus on actions that cause you to hit the ball. When you practice, or play a match that you consider practice, your mind can observe what you're doing and compare your observations to what you are striving to achieve. You can mentally focus on how your tennis "feels."

When you reflect on your tennis off the court or during practice, you may *think* about or analyze the way you play. You may decide, for example, that you need to employ more topspin or mix up your shots.

But when you play to win, don't be observing or thinking or feeling. Be focused on reacting to your opponent's shots and on hitting the ball.

Winning at tennis boils down ultimately to how you hit each ball. Hit the ball well every time, and you'll play well. That means concentration should be on playing each ball, not each point, not each game. Not on *where* to hit each ball. Just on hitting it. Hit each ball well and the points and games will take care of themselves. That also simplifies what you have to concentrate on.

Another way to view concentration in tennis is to distinguish between actions and results. The right way to concentrate is to focus on actions. The wrong way is to think about results. Reacting, making your racket hit the ball and recovering from your last shot are actions. These are specific things that you can *do*.

When hitting, you do not want to concentrate—even for a split second—on such thoughts as winning this point or putting the ball into the open court. Those thoughts do nothing to help you hit the ball. They are not actions; they are desired results, wishes, goals.

The way to achieve results is to concentrate on the actions that cause them.

You Won't Concentrate Like A
Pro Unless You Are One

Tournament and other advanced players have hit so many balls that they don't need to concentrate in the same way that you and I do. Hitting the ball with the racket's sweetspot, for example, has become so natural to them that they can put their minds to other aspects of the game—like tactics. Where is the best spot to hit the next ball? What kind of pace and spin can they put on the ball that will disrupt their opponents' play?

Most of us, however, cannot expect to win that way. Remember when you first learned to drive an automobile? Your attention was focused almost exclusively on keeping the car in your own lane and maintaining the right speed. Now you do that naturally, enabling you to turn part of your attention to other conditions and happenings on the road that could affect you.

It could be said that as an accomplished driver you're able to spend some of your time on road tactics, just as advanced players are expert enough to devote some of their attention to tennis tactics.

Accomplished tennis players keep the ball on the court

Different Forms of Concentration

There are times you play to win, and times you play to practice. Your mental activities will be different for each.

When you practice, your mind will be paying attention to what you are practicing. You might be focusing on timing, or on your racket position as it meets the ball, or other aspects of the physical game. Or you might focus on what your thoughts are as you hit the ball. Then you'd be paying attention to the mental game. You'd be concentrating on how you concentrate.

When you compete, however, your mind should not be on exploring either the physical or mental game. Your full attention should be on the actions needed to hit the ball.

while simultaneously paying some attention to their opponents, to ball placement, to deception and perhaps more. Don't expect to do the same until you've played so much that hitting the ball solidly is as natural as driving your car down the road. When you have reached that point then you can turn part of your attention to tactics.

Your concentration will be sporadic if you try focusing on too much at the same time. If, in addition to trying to be aware of the ball, you are also thinking about your opponent, the open court, where you should be positioned and whether you should hit to your opponent's backhand as well as keeping a firm wrist and moving your feet, you are going to end up confused. Your play will be erratic.

The trick is to focus on the one or two actions that are most effective for you. Do so on each and every hit. You will need to learn what those actions are for you. For most of us, the first action is to react to your opponent's shot, and the second is to make your racket hit the ball.

5

Concentrating on the Big Two: Reacting and Hitting

OF ALL THE TASKS THAT YOUR CONCENTRATION IS CALLED upon to perform in tennis, the most important is making sure that your racket meets the ball squarely. But it isn't the first. Before you can hit your opponent's shot you must react to it—even when the ball is on the other side of the net.

Reacting is an action that occurs as soon as your *opponent* hits. Making your racket meet the ball is an action that occurs as *you* hit. If you are going to think about only two elements of tennis during competitive play (what you think about during practice is another matter), they should be reacting to your opponent's shot and making your racket meet the ball.

I say "make your *racket* meet the ball" —instead of simply "hit the ball" —because I want your mind focused on the racket as well as the ball. You're less likely to be distracted by the open court, for example, if you are committed to the racket and ball meeting. Focusing on "hit the ball" allows the associated distraction of "to where."

Reacting

One of the most powerful breakthroughs you can experience will come from your exploration of reacting. Reacting is a more powerful concept than "be ready," the usual advice. Being ready usually means assuming some "ready" position with your hands and feet. That causes you to stand a certain way. I want you to *move*, not stand.

The instant your opponent hits the ball, concentrate on the ball's flight and getting your racket on it—not on anything else. Not on your swing, not on keeping a firm wrist, not on being ready, not on winning the point, not on watching the ball, not on anything but *getting to the ball*.

Let the ball determine what you do. You don't control your opponent's shot, so you must react to the ball. This is not something you've been told to do in tennis lessons. But what is reacting? How do you do it?

Watching the Ball Won't Do It

Simply watching the ball will not make it go over the net. Your racket needs to hit it. The racket and ball must meet. So your concentration must include not only the ball but the racket as well.

Of course you can't watch both the ball and the racket, at least not with your eyes. But you can watch the ball with your eyes while you focus your mind on the racket meeting it.

Concentration involves the mind and the eyes. Concentrate on making the racket hit the ball, and you won't need to think about watching the ball. That will be automatic. It's a natural part of hitting.

You perform an action better if you focus on the action instead of the result of the action. A surgeon focuses on the action of his scalpel making a clean incision, and not on how the incision will look when it's completed.

Reacting is a physical action, but following a series of physical steps will not help you react. What does help is to *mentally* focus on the act of reacting. Just tell yourself to react and your body will take care of the rest, with the right physical actions following.

Concentrating on getting to the ball will make you start quicker, run faster and swing sooner. These achievements will not happen simply through watching the ball, nor through "being ready." Only the determination to react to the ball—to get your racket on it—will work. That determination makes you watch the ball, be ready for the ball, move to intercept the ball, swing at the ball with the right timing, and attack the ball. After you hit, start concentrating on reacting again. That will get you to move to cover the open court, and to be alert to what your opponent is doing.

Competition Is Not Like Practice

When you practice, your practice partner hits the ball to you with the idea of keeping it in play. That gives you time to be aware of getting into position, as well as to observe the timing of your swing, your balance, and the act of meeting the ball.

In a match, on the other hand, your opponent usually hits the ball so that you can't get to it easily, so that you're rushed or out of position. In situations such as these your attention, emphasis and concentration should be on one thing and one thing only: reacting to the ball. You don't have time for perfect strokes.

To stroke perfectly you have to hit with the right swing from the right position. More often than not you won't be able to get in the right position and you won't have time to swing properly, either. If perfect strokes are your top priority, you are going to find yourself losing to less graceful but scrappy players whose first concern is getting to the ball, no matter how.

Better to concentrate on swinging whatever way is possible, given the time you have, than to try to swing your perfect swing. Swing the way you need to in order to hit the ball. React to the ball, no matter where it is going or how it is hit.

If your opponent hits a short ball, reacting promptly will provide you with time to *attack* the ball, to step into it and hit it with authority. Attacking makes life difficult for your opponent. You will return the ball sooner, giving him less time to react. And when you attack you take less time to set up for your stroke, so you're less likely to telegraph where your ball is going.

Hitting

As soon as you've reacted, begin to focus on the hit itself. Concentrate on driving the racket's sweetspot through the ball. Concentrate on that on every shot you hit—groundstrokes, serves, volleys, overheads, half-volleys—all of them.

Let's zero in on this. It's crucial.

We've already noted that when you practice or warm up,

Attacking Is a Frame of Mind

"Attacking" in tennis means reacting to the ball in such a way that you're able to swing at the ball fully. Get yourself into an attacking frame of mind and wonderful things begin to take place.

First, you focus on the ball's motion. That's better than simply watching it. Focusing on the ball makes it more likely you'll hit it cleanly.

Second, concentrating on a controlled attack of the ball increases the odds that you'll hit through the ball.

Third, you tend to respond sooner and more aggressively, with your feet moving naturally as part of the attack. That's preferable to the time-consuming process of your brain analyzing the unfolding play and telling your feet where to move.

---

you have the time to set up for the perfect stroke because your partner is trying to hit the ball right to you.

But not only is your partner hitting the ball to you, you're hitting it back to him in much the same fashion. You're not trying to put it away; you're trying to keep it in play. You are, however, interested in hitting the ball well and the friendly ball exchanges during practice are just right for that.

Without the pressure of competition you're not distracted. In practice your mind is free to concentrate on nothing else but making the racket hit the ball squarely. Did you ever wonder why a wonderful warm-up was followed by disastrous play after the match started?

The answer isn't complicated. When you play a match you're likely to become result-oriented; instead of focusing on the ball and impact, you start concentrating on where you want the ball to go or how you want to win. Consequently, you mis-hit more often.

In competition, learn to keep your mind focused on making the racket hit the ball instead of where you want the ball to go. Interestingly, if you do, more balls will go where you'd like them to. That's because, as we discussed, you are concentrating on the *action* needed, instead of the result wanted.

In those matches when nothing seems to work, check whether your eyes and mind are focused at impact on your racket meeting the ball. If you're like me, you'll find that too often they're not.

It takes a lot of practice to change that habit. But it's rewarding when you do.

How to Watch the Ball

At the moment of hitting, "watch the ball" won't do as an order to yourself. You must "make the racket hit the ball." Still, part of hitting involves watching the ball. What does that mean? It means becoming aware of the ball's speed and depth as it approaches. You need to do that to react properly. Estimate where it will bounce so your reaction to the ball gets you into a good hitting position. Be aware of the ball's spin, as that will affect its bounce. Watch the ball so you can get into a position to make your racket meet it.

If it's a very short ball, or a very wide ball, be aware of where it will bounce its *second* bounce. That way you'll find you have more time to hit than you think. Your racket only has to reach the ball before it bounces twice. Being aware of the second bounce helps you get many balls your opponent thinks you can't reach. People who get to seemingly impossible shots know where the second bounce will be.

Those Last Two Feet

Watching the ball seems easy. You watch it clear the net, watch it arc through the air and watch it bounce on your side. You are sure you're following the universal sports adage: "Keep your eye on the ball." But often you stop watching it when you swing.

Avoid that by being particularly alert to those last two feet the ball travels before it reaches you. That will help you stay focused on the impact. But don't only watch the ball. Be conscious of the racket *and* the ball. Sense the racket meeting the ball solidly.

Sensing the Racket

You "see" the racket with your mind, not your eyes. You can only observe the racket with your mind through the sensations it receives from the nerves in your hand and arms. That means you feel the racket and the motion of your body and racket, your "hitting system." So when I say make the racket meet the ball, I mean you need to see the ball's motion, and feel your racket moving to hit it. When you practice, be conscious of the feel of the racket moving toward the ball. That will help you develop your timing. Of course, when you play, just focus on the impact itself, not on the feeling of the swing.

6

What Else to Concentrate On . . . and Not to Concentrate On

OFTEN YOU COMMIT ERRORS NOT BECAUSE YOU HAVE NOT been concentrating, but because you've been concentrating on the wrong things.

Concentrate On the Ball, Not the Point

Don't concentrate on winning points. It distracts you from concentrating on hitting the ball.

Ignore the tennis tip "play tough on the big points." It sounds pithy, but standing by itself it's meaningless. How do you play tough? What exactly do you concentrate on? What should your eyes watch and mind pay attention to? What actions do you take to play tough?

For many it means "try harder." Does that mean to run faster and hit harder? Does it require hitting differently from how you have been?

Bjorn Borg was quoted once as saying he played the big points the same way he played every other point.

I interpret that to mean that if you think about playing tough on the big points, it will distract you from what you always should be doing—getting to and hitting the ball.

If for no other reason, concentration should be the same on all points because that simplifies your game. You unnecessarily complicate your concentration if you need to think differently about big points, ordinary points, game points, and match points.

Beware of Aiming

We all would like to get the ball to where our opponent isn't. That's one sure way to win points. But the fact is that focusing too much on hitting to the open court is a mistake. More often than not we'll mis-hit the ball because we tried to aim it somewhere. Being distracted by the wish to hit to the open court prevents concentration on the actions involved in hitting the ball.

According to the Zen master cited by Eugen Herrigal in *Zen in the Art of Archery*, the reason the student cannot hit the target is because he keeps trying to hit the target. The student would do better to pay attention to perfecting how he pulls the bowstring, grips the bow, and releases the string. These are actions. Hitting the target is a result.

Similarly in tennis, aiming the ball—even unconsciously—creates at least three difficulties. One is obvious: you tend to look at your target, taking your eye off the ball and increasing the likelihood you'll mis-hit. The second is that, even if your eyes are on the ball, your mind may be on the target and not on the action of making the racket meet the ball. The third difficulty is more complicated.

If you aim at a certain point, such as the open court, you must get yourself not only in a position to meet the ball but into a position so that the ball goes where you're aiming.

If, however, you focus solely on hitting the ball, you need only get into a position to meet the ball rather than meet it and put it somewhere specific. You are faced with one task, not two. Moreover, it is easier to get into position to simply hit the ball than to line yourself up in a position to hit the ball to a specific area.

Let the ball decide what shot you'll make. Don't think about what you need to do—such as getting the ball back, passing your opponent or aiming—and focus only on the ball and your racket hitting it. So what if the ball goes straight at your opponent? There's a good chance it will be so well-hit that the best he can manage is a run-of-the-mill return.

This is not to say there aren't occasions when aiming is appropriate. If the opportunity beckons—your opponent, for example, has left one side of the court completely uncovered—and you have the time, you can decide to put the ball in the open court.

But that decision is made *before* you start the hitting process. And once it is made, *get it out of your mind*. Concentrate exclusively on the ball and the hit. Your body will have received the message and will do what has to be done to get the ball where you want it.

Don't Be Too Concerned with Tactics

Tactics are great for the advanced player. They are the bane of the rest of us.

Thoughts on tactics crowd out your concentration when you hit the ball. Tactics are for players who already possess excellent control and concentration. Ivan Lendl can make his tactics work. Most of us, when we get too tactical, mis-hit the ball. The tactics would have been great—if we had been able to execute them.

Better to put a well-hit ball over the net in the center of the court than to mis-hit what *would have been* a dazzling winner along the sideline. How many times has your doubles partner said "You had the right idea" after you'd missed a delicate tactical ploy and lost the point?

Concentrate on "DO's," Not on "DON'T's"

Several years ago I played two doubles tournament matches on the same day, a day on which I was playing poorly. Each of my partners tried to help me—in different ways. One worked, the other didn't.

My first partner kept saying: "Don't be intimidated." My second partner told me: "Move your feet." We lost the match I played with partner one. Partner two and I won.

Moving my feet was affirmative. It was something I could

Stop Saying "Just Get the Ball Back"

Sometimes results sound like actions. In doubles, for example, you will hear someone tell his partner, "Just get it back." We often say that to ourselves when we're in a tough match, missing service returns.

That's counterproductive. Getting the ball back is a wish, not an action. The action you really need to take is get the sweetspot of your racket to meet the ball. That will make the ball go back most of the time.

It puts a lot of pressure on your partner to say "Just get it back." If he or she doesn't, it's another failure and makes the next return even more difficult.

Do your partner a favor. Let him know that he needn't worry about getting it back. Tell him that the only thing both of you should be doing is to simply hit every ball. Whether or not they go in isn't important.

---

do. It was something I could specifically concentrate *on*.

"Don't be intimidated," on the other hand, gave me nothing to focus on. It gave me something not to do but gave no hints on how not to do it. It didn't tell me what to concentrate on to keep from being intimidated.

In the heat of play, concentration needs to be focused on actions that are doable.

"Don't be nervous," "don't hit to his backhand," and "don't be intimidated" are all "don't's." They are not actions to concentrate on. They distract you from hitting the ball.

"Watch your opponent's moves," "make your racket hit the ball," "recover," "react to the ball" are all actions you *do*. Note these are all directed toward helping you hit the next ball.

Avoid Other Distractions

Concentration is not as easy as it might appear. Too many other thoughts get in the way. The basics of the physical game, balance, timing and the like, may well be worthwhile thoughts to dwell on during practice but they don't belong in your mind during a match. You develop them through exploration during practice with the eventual aim of having them become part of your muscle memory. That means your body will automatically execute them without your mind focusing on them.

But if your mind dwells on technique during a match, you will likely be thinking about such mechanical steps as:

"Get sideways to the net."

"Be sure to follow through."

"Keep a firm wrist."

Thinking about results also gets in the way:

"I'll hit it to the open court."

"I'll lob it over his head."

"This one's a put-away."

And then there are those hidden and not-so-hidden concerns about self-image:

"That's the third return I've missed, I can imagine what my partner is thinking."

"Game point. Am I going to blow it?"

"Here I go, I'm going to lose to him again."

All of these will cost you games if you think about them during a match.

The way to concentrate on what you should is to become aware of your thoughts as you play. Find out what your mind and eyes focus on. Become good at recalling what your mind was doing when you *missed* the shot. Most of us soon find that too often we do not focus on the actions that make a difference, like on hitting when you're hitting. If you're aiming when you should be hitting, become aware of that. Over time, this awareness will cause a change in your concentration from being distracted to being focused on the two physical components that you are supposed to concentrate on during a match— reacting and hitting.

"Imaging" and Tennis

Much has been written in the field of motivation about the use of "imaging" as a means of helping to attain results. Some have applied it to tennis. I have no argument with the theory but if you want to employ it, be sure you understand when to use it.

If you visualize yourself winning the club championship it might well motivate you to practice, exercise, diet and take similar steps that actually will increase your chances of winning. But if you "image" yourself winning as you hit the ball, I guarantee you will mis-hit the ball more often than not. Visualizations such as these tend to distract you from the task at hand.

Said another way, imaging may help you between matches, between games and even between points, but don't do it while you're hitting! For example, you can visualize a perfect serve before starting your service motion, but once you start your serve, keep your mind on making a perfect impact.

7

What to Concentrate on When You're Not Hitting

MANY TENNIS PLAYERS CONCENTRATE WELL WHEN THEY'RE hitting but still manage to lose points through lack of concentration. How is that possible? Easy. They fail to concentrate during those moments when they're *not* hitting.

What you concentrate on when you're not hitting obviously is less critical than when you are hitting. Nonetheless, there are specific actions you should be focusing on at these times. A failure to do so can hurt.

Essentially, there are two non-hitting moments during which concentration plays an important part.

As You Recover

The first takes place right after you've hit the ball. You want to make sure that you have the court covered to handle your opponent's return. In other words, be aware of where he might put the ball. More likely than not, it will be in the open court. So be aware of the court you left open when you hit, and try to cover it.

After you've recovered from your stroke, concentrate on moving. You'll be tempted to watch where your ball lands, but tennis isn't golf; you don't have that luxury. Play doesn't stop. Your job is to get ready for the next ball coming at you, and the first thing to do after you've hit is to start moving.

Moving at this point is so critical that moving in *any* direction is preferable to standing there flat-footed waiting for your opponent's return. Somehow your eyes, your body and your mind work together so that you usually will go in the right direction. Besides, getting on your toes and moving heightens your ability to react to the ball that soon will be coming over the net.

As Your Opponent Starts to Hit

The second key non-hitting moment takes place after you've recovered and have started moving. Now you want to begin focusing on your opponent. It will be easier to get to the ball if you can tell where your opponent is likely to hit it.

While that is often the open court, it could also be an area of the court you're leaving, "off footing" you. Prepare for this eventuality by watching your opponent's swing closely.

If his feet seem lined up to hit to your forehand, ready yourself for a forehand. The same with backhands. But don't let yourself become too analytical in these observations; it may well confuse you if you do. Sometimes just being *aware* of the question of where he might hit is enough to get you moving in the right direction. Like other aspects of awareness, somehow it produces the result you want even though you can't point your finger to anything specific you've figured out.

Concentrating on your opponent's actions just before he hits can also provide you with a warning of a drop shot or a lob. Similarly, by observing your opponent's swing you can often tell how the ball will bounce when it reaches your side of the court. Is your opponent going through the kind of motions that produce topspin? How hard is he swinging? Did he hit from deep in the court, or will he hit an approach shot off your short ball?

His actions are important. They affect the way you begin to react for your next hit. Pay attention to them. Again, don't feel you have to dissect what's going on—just be aware of it.

If this is more than you feel you can handle at your stage of play, then simply keep watching the ball when your opponent is hitting. "Watch the ball" is adequate advice in that case. But as you improve, you can begin to pay more attention to your opponent's shot-making.

8

The Key to Winning:
Don't Be Afraid of Losing

YOU OFTEN LOSE IN TENNIS BECAUSE YOU ARE CONCENTRAT-
ing too much on winning—winning points, winning games,
winning in general.

The key to winning is not to be afraid of losing.

There's nothing wrong with a *desire* to win. It's an *obses-
sion* with winning that causes problems, and it inflicts damage
at two levels.

The first level deals with specific shots. Too often the *need*
to win makes you intent on placing the ball in a difficult spot or
putting the ball away. You're concentrating on where the ball
will be going or what you will be doing to it.

You ought to be concentrating on the present, focusing on
the ball and only the ball, caring not about its future but only
about making solid contact. Forget about aiming. Your body
and mind, working together, will instinctively know where in
your opponent's court to put the ball.

The second level involves overall attitude about winning
or, to be more accurate, the fear of losing. It concerns image.

Even though you *know* you should be focusing on hitting the ball instead of putting it somewhere, you find it hard to do just that time after time. That's because there's a bigger mental game going on than tennis, and it has to do with image. With looking good. It mostly happens in matches you "should" win, or when you're ahead 5-1 in the third.

Think back for a moment. Try to recall what was in your mind when you didn't play well. The truth is that you don't play well when you are thinking about how you are doing and how your performance stacks up with your expectations for yourself. Such thoughts can creep into the back of your mind and undermine your play even when you are trying to concentrate on hitting.

Detach "Good" and "Bad" From Winning and Losing

This is not a book on psychology. Nonetheless I urge you to explore a philosophical concept that has made an enormous difference for me, and can for you too.

I believe it's human nature to attach meanings to winning and losing. When you win, you tell yourself "I look good." When you lose, it's "I look bad." (For the moment withhold judgment on whether or not you think what I'm saying is true or not. Just stick with me and explore the concept.)

Does winning or losing at tennis really mean anything? Yes, they mean something if you're a professional and your livelihood depends on winning. But for most of us, whether we win or lose really doesn't mean anything to anyone but ourselves. My losing doesn't mean nearly as much to someone else as it too often does to me. If I attach the meaning "I look bad" to losing, then I'll be afraid of losing and will play badly.

While losing may not be fun, it doesn't have to mean "I'm lousy." It needn't affect my self-image unless I allow it to do so. Losing should mean I lost—nothing more.

Let go of the *need* to win, and you'll be able to concentrate on hitting the ball. What *will* mean something to you is playing well, and then anyone who beats you will know they played well. A sense of tennis integrity enters the game. Playing becomes more important than the results of playing.

Winning Is Still More Fun

I am not saying you shouldn't care if you win or lose. The desire to win should be strong and the result of winning fun. That's different, though, from attaching meaning or significance to the final score. Fun and desire are emotions, not conclusions. "I should have won" is a conclusion. You're passing judgment on yourself.

Choking

The negative meaning you attach to losing can cause you to choke. Instead of concentrating on play, you become self-conscious and embarrassed. But if you attach no meaning to losing, then choking and playing poorly will not control your thoughts.

Simply being *aware* of this concept will enable you from time to time to avoid the pitfalls of self-destructive thoughts. But if you want it to work all of the time, you've got to do more than intellectually recognize its validity. *Knowing* what works will not help as much *doing* what works. Understanding is not enough. You must become someone to whom losing is truly meaningless, rather than someone who merely understands it to be meaningless.

How Do You Get There?

I can promise you that this approach to winning works. But only you can allow yourself to stop attaching meaning to losing so that the fear of losing stops holding you back. You start by

accepting the possibility that this is an area worth exploring—
that there is a breakthrough available here—and explore it.

It takes time, just as it takes time to improve other components of tennis that involve a combination of mental discipline
and physical action.

In my own experience, I found that by eliminating the
importance of losing I also eliminated the importance of winning. What took the place of both was the importance of being
able to play well. Tennis became genuinely fun when I saw
every ball coming at me as another opportunity to feel the joy of
hitting. And when hitting instead of winning became the goal, I
hit better and started winning.

PART THREE

THE
PHYSICAL
GAME:
THE
JOYFUL
ONE

THE MENTAL GAME IS CRUCIAL TO PLAYING winning tennis. Nonetheless, tennis is a physical activity. The reason we are out there on the court is because of the physical joy and benefits that we draw from it.

In the following section you will read about the physical components of tennis that must be mastered if you are to play well. They include the *basics*, which consist primarily of how to position yourself to hit the ball plus the essential concepts of *timing* and *balance*. How well you employ these elements determines the effectiveness of your *strokes*.

Some of what you will learn fits in with conventional tennis teaching methods and will be familiar to you. Most of it flies in the face of what is traditionally taught.

But all of it is based on sound reasoning.

And it works, especially for those who have had limited success in taking the usual learning path.

9

But First a Word About Basics

CERTAIN TENNIS MECHANICS MUST BE BUILT INTO YOUR muscle memory.

Yes, I know this sounds like a blatant violation of the *Breakthrough Tennis* philosophy, which rejects a mechanical, standardized approach to the game. But consider these few directives as physical fundamentals, so basic and general that they apply uniformly to just about everybody. You may already be satisfied that you have these fundamentals down; only you can be the judge. If you have any doubts whatsoever, keep in mind that mastering these basics will better allow you to develop the non-mechanical aspects of the physical game—timing and balance—as well as concentration.

The real breakthroughs in your physical game will come from exploring timing and balance. But before you can explore them, you must be able to position yourself to swing at a ball. Correct positioning means, essentially, using a compact swing, stepping into the ball and hitting well out in front of you.

To explore these fundamentals of positioning, it is useful to break them up into specific *actions*.

Hitting Out in Front

It's important—in fact it's crucial—that your racket meet the ball at the right moment and the right place. Hitting at the right moment involves timing and we'll get to that in a later chapter. But hitting at the right place means hitting the ball at the correct spot relative to your body, and if you fail to do that you'll disrupt both your timing and your balance.

You hit at the wrong place if you meet the ball too early or too late. A player who hits too early finds himself stretching forward awkwardly as he hits. Few players hit too early. Hitting late, which is common among beginners and intermediates, means meeting the ball when it's almost past you. If you hit a forehand late you're hitting it with your racket near your hip or even further back. Hitting late also means the ball is past the point at which you can see it best.

The right place to hit is *out in front of your torso, wherever it is facing*. This definition may sound odd but it accurately describes what I'm trying to get across. If you can't visualize it, don't worry. It's one of those concepts easier to execute than to imagine in the abstract.

Swinging a racket in your living room should help. Going out on the court and actually hitting balls will make even clearer what I'm trying to tell you.

Whatever you have to do, it's important that you get it right. Nothing hinders your game more than failing to meet the ball well out in front of you. No stroke can feel right until the impact point is right.

Because people take different stances when they swing, "out in front" will not appear to mean the same thing to everyone. Some players turn completely sideways to the net to hit, while others almost face the net. Most are somewhere in between. And many players take different stances depending on the stroke they're employing.

Think of the way you swing—I don't care what stroke. At the moment of impact between the racket and the ball, your torso *will* be facing some direction. Look at the accompanying illustrations as you read this. Note that with each shot the ball is met more or less in the direction the torso is facing. The direction your torso faces is where "out in front" is for you. If you turn sideways to hit, then at impact your torso will face more toward the sideline, and the sideline will be in the direction of "out in front." If you are turned not quite so far, and you're facing one of the netposts, then the netpost will be in the direction of "out in front."

The definition even applies to players who take a stance facing directly into the net. If you watch them carefully, you'll notice that just as they start their swing they twist their shoulders and torso at a 45-degree angle and end up facing toward one of the netposts. At impact the ball is "out in front" of them.

I'm talking about direction, not height. If the ball is a high volley, "out in front" is chest high, but still in the direction your torso points.

How Far Away Should You Be From the Ball?

Most people are too close to the ball when they hit. You should be far enough away so that you can step toward the ball and still have your arm comfortably extended at impact. The elbow should be slightly bent. The accompanying illustrations show the correct arm extension.

Practicing and Exploring Hitting Out in Front

When you practice, experiment with moving into a position where ball impact occurs "out in front" of you. It's good physics. If your racket face is in front of you, your wrist will be cocked open in the correct "fixed wrist" position. "Cocked

Hitting out in front. In each stroke, the ball is met more or less in front of the torso. Note how the hitting arm is freely extended away from the body.

open" means your wrist is bent back about 45 degrees from your forearm. (It is shown in the illustration demonstrating the forehand stroke.)

If you meet the ball in front of you, after impact the racket will naturally follow through in the direction you want the ball to go. Because you won't be pulling the racket across the ball you will experience fewer mis-hits. Your wrist will stay fixed— cocked open—through the whole swing, taking away the source of errors.

And going straight through the ball means the full force of your swing goes in the same direction as the ball. That produces more power.

Whatever else you do, be conscious of hitting so that you comfortably meet the ball well out in front of you. More than anything else, it's what separates advanced players from inter- mediates, as it allows hitting with good timing.

Make the Ball Rise

Hitting the ball out in front doesn't guarantee that it will clear the net. To do that you've got to make the ball rise when you hit it. If the ball easily clears the net and lands deep in your opponent's court, he will be limited in what he can do with it. Most intermediates hit balls that barely clear the net and land short. This allows their opponents to move toward the ball,

Make the ball rise at impact. In the top sequence, the ball is hit with an upward drive of the legs to produce topspin. The racket face is vertical at impact.

which is the preferred way to approach a shot.

How much the ball rises, where it lands and what kind of bounce the ball takes depends on two factors: the tilt of your racket face and the kind of movement you apply to your racket. These also determine the type of spin the ball takes.

If the racket face is tilted upward slightly and the racket comes slightly *under* the ball, the ball will rise with underspin. The upward tilt deflects the ball upward to easily clear the net.

In the lower sequence, the racket starts high but comes under the ball, with the slight upward tilt of the racket producing underspin.

Creating underspin is fairly easy for most people because the stroke required is a relatively natural one.

Making the ball rise at impact by creating topspin is harder. You achieve topspin by holding the racket face straight up and down—perpendicular to the ground—and moving the racket upward at impact, brushing upward on the ball. Done correctly, the ball will land deep in your opponent's court and bounce high, making it difficult to return.

But topspin is a two-edged sword. It takes much more energy to hit with topspin than it does with underspin. To achieve topspin you must drive upward with your legs, which means first bending deeply at the knees. The down-up knee action takes energy. Hitting with topspin time after time requires strong legs. Obviously as one ages generating topspin can become more arduous. In the National 50's, for example, you see much less topspin than in matches for younger age groups. The best senior players use efficient strokes with little topspin. Young, stronger players can afford the extra energy required by extreme topspin. But if they've relied exclusively on topspin they may not be among the top seeds when they reach their 50's.

The accompanying illustrations should help in understanding spin.

For some people, the best stroke is hit with little or no spin at all—neither underspin or topspin. You can achieve that by tilting your racket face back a small amount and hitting slightly upward. Or to put it another way, come slightly up from under the ball. This leads to an efficient shot. You will not need to swing hard to get good pace. All the swing energy goes into the ball's pace instead of into generating spin. That means you won't wear yourself out, especially if you're not in great physical condition.

Whatever stroke you use, the ball needs to be lofted to clear the net. It's a good thing to keep in mind as you practice. Try to err on the side of hitting balls long rather than into the net. I once watched two intermediates play a set and kept count of how points were lost. Thirty-two were lost by hitting into the net; seven by hitting long.

Hit Through the Ball

One of the most important elements in hitting well is to *hit through the ball*. Too many players simply meet the ball. That's not enough. When you do, the tendency is to stop your swing early and let the wrist flop through. Hitting through the ball means to drive the racket strings well beyond the impact point. A good deal of your swing should occur after the impact. That will give you power, and prevent the wristy shots that make you inconsistent. This is often called follow-through.

You hit through the ball by accelerating the racket through the impact point. (This acceleration is part of developing your timing; more will be said of it when we discuss timing in detail.) Envision your swing as an arc. Think of pulling the racket through so that more than half of the arc develops *after* the impact point. That is what is meant by follow-through, but I prefer to say "hit through the ball" because it keeps your mental focus on the impact itself instead of on the racket's motion.

Move Toward the Ball to Hit

We're better at moving forward than we are at moving sideways or backward. You're far quicker—you react faster—if you move forward to intercept the ball as it approaches, if you attack it.

Moving forward to intercept the ball makes it likely you'll step into the ball as you hit. That generates more power. You're moving the same direction as your racket, the direction you want the ball to go.

To see how important moving forward is to reacting, try this next time you practice: Ask your practice partner to hit you serves, hard serves. Stand a few feet deeper than usual to receive them. Just before he hits his serve, do something contrary to what you may be doing now. Abandon your natural inclination to backpedal in anticipation of a powerful serve and instead start moving *forward*. As you move forward, intercept the ball with your racket. Be determined to meet the ball no matter where or how hard it is hit.

You'll be surprised how well you meet the ball, especially a fast-moving ball. The reason isn't complicated. Starting to move forward before your opponent hits the ball guarantees that you won't be flat-footed when you start to swing. Moving forward helps you react. You won't need to swing hard because your forward motion will provide power. You can simply block the hard serve.

Once you've reached the point where you're comfortable with that technique for the service return, try it on other shots. For example, moving forward to intercept the ball makes you much quicker on volleys. If the situation allows it, moving forward even helps you hit overheads.

Step Into the Ball

"Moving toward the ball" helps you reach the ball. "Stepping into the ball" affects the power of your shot rather than your ability to reach the ball.

If you've reacted well and therefore positioned yourself soon enough to hit aggressively, then you'll hit with more power if you begin your swing by stepping forward. That means your weight will be moving into your shot as you hit. Stepping forward is a fundamental in many sports. A baseball player steps forward when hitting and when throwing. A boxer steps forward to throw a punch. In all cases it produces power to bring the weight of the body into play.

You may need to experiment with this a bit. Practice getting your swing to include stepping into the ball.

Notice that I did not say "make yourself step into the ball when you swing." Don't force yourself to step into the ball. Instead, work on developing a swing that includes stepping forward. It's a cause-and-effect difference: stepping forward should be thought of as the result of a good swing, not its cause.

Use a Shorter Swing for Timing, Control and Power

One of the first lessons a tennis beginner is taught is to bring his racket back before he swings—way back. When he finally swings he is supposed to make a wide arc that stretches from his extended racket behind him to the follow-through point in front. It's one of the cardinal rules of tennis.

Ignore it.

I want you instead to consider developing a compact swing.

Think of driving a large nail into the side of a fencepost. The nail is waist high and you're swinging a hammer (much like hitting a forehand) to hit the nailhead. If you take the hammer back in a very long arc behind you and then swing it forward, you'll almost surely miss the nail.

On the other hand if you bring the hammer back in a shorter, compact arc and then swing it forward, you'll usually hit the nail squarely. If, in addition, you swing the hammer with your torso, and not just your arm, you join your body's momentum with the hammer's weight. Then each accurate hit will be more powerful.

It's the same when you hit a tennis ball. A short, compact swing of the body is more accurate and more powerful than a long, loose swing of the arm from the shoulder.

Develop your swing so it's compact.

Putting It All Together

Think of tossing a 10-pound sack of potatoes into the back of a pickup truck. You hold the sack with two hands, bring it back a little, step forward and release it in front of your torso with an upward motion. That motion includes most of the basics of a forehand tennis swing. Just substitute your racket for the sack of potatoes.

In a good swing you hold the racket in front of you, bring it back a little, step into the ball as you swing the racket upward, meeting the ball just in front of your belly button.

Note that when you toss the potato sack, both your hands work together. The same works in tennis. Your hands are naturally together on a two-handed backhand since they hold the racket. But keeping your hands fairly close together works on the one-handed forehand as well. While your left hand is not on the racket, you keep it in front of you, a few inches from the hitting hand. As you turn your shoulders, both hands come back together. As you swing, both go forward together. Your hands working together keep you in balance.

The potato sack analogy also demonstrates why bringing your racket way back is not necessary and may even be counterproductive. You would not bring the sack of potatoes way back behind you to toss it. Instead, you'd bring it back about to your thigh and then step forward to get power as you throw. That's the way to get power into your shots, too.

10

Timing and Skinny Twelve-Year-Olds

IF YOU'VE SWUNG A CHILD ON A PLAYGROUND SWING, YOU understand timing. You wouldn't push when the swing is still coming toward you, nor stop it at the top of its arc and then let it go. Those disrupt the rhythm. Instead, you help the swing move its own natural way.

Learn to help your racket and body—your hitting system—swing that way too.

How Timing Affects Your Tennis Game

Timing is what enables a skinny 12-year-old girl to hit the ball harder than a 200-pound man whacking away with all his might. The adult fights against himself. The youngster simply helps the racket along. Her muscles aren't strong enough to do otherwise.

Timing means swinging your entire hitting system—the combination of body, arm, and racket—so smoothly that the full force of your momentum is transferred to the ball with little effort.

Your timing is right when you hit the ball perfectly. You use little effort, yet the ball zings over the net deep and hard. We've all felt those efficient shots. Some days we hit many of them, on others, very few. The aim is to hit all balls with perfect timing.

Hit 100 balls in practice, and count how many you hit that way. Most of us hit fewer than half of them on the racket's sweetspot, and only a few of those are hit with the perfect timing that drives the ball off the strings with pace. An intermediate player will hit less than 10 percent of his or her shots with good timing. Lack of timing costs you points. It also robs you of tennis satisfaction, which is even more important.

When your game is off, check your timing.

Pendulums and Momentum

The weight on a grandfather's clock—the pendulum—swings smoothly back and forth with perfect timing. Learn to swing that way. Your hitting system—racket, arm, and body—is like the clock's pendulum. Pendulums obey Newton's Laws of Motion. Good timing depends on Newton's Laws, so we should obey them, too.

Every pendulum has its own natural timing, which depends on the pendulum's length and mass. A long pendulum swings slowly. A long *heavy* pendulum swings slower yet, but has more momentum. Momentum puts power in your shot. Momentum is defined as *mass* times *velocity*. So to get more power, you can either swing faster, or use more mass. Think of the huge wrecking balls swung from construction cranes to demolish buildings. Wrecking balls swing very slowly, but with enormous momentum.

Your body, arm, and racket comprise a more complicated pendulum than a clock or a wrecking ball, but the concepts of timing and momentum still apply. When your timing is right, you swing the racket back and then forward to hit the ball, much like the clock pendulum swings one way, then the other.

But you don't swing just the racket. You swing your arm, or your arm and shoulders, or your whole body, along with the racket. You swing different masses—different hitting systems—depending on the shot you're making.

The difference between people and the clock pendulum is that people have muscles, which in tennis can be a disadvantage. Muscles can be used to force your hitting system to swing in unnatural rhythms. When your timing is right, your muscles help your hitting system swing naturally. When it's off, your muscles force it to swing unnaturally. That's why skinny 12-year-olds often have relatively good timing. Their weak muscles aren't as likely to force the racket to swing unnaturally.

Momentum Comes From Your Body, Not Your Racket

On groundstrokes, your racket is not the main source of the momentum transferred to the ball. Your arm, or better yet, your arm and body, are.

I'm an average-sized man. My right arm weighs about ten pounds while my racket weighs less than one pound. When I hit the ball, my arm produces a lot more momentum than my racket.

If I swing all of my body weight along with my arm and racket, I generate even more momentum.

In other words, don't swing just the racket when you explore power hitting. Explore power by feeling the swing of your entire hitting system: racket, arm, torso and legs combined.

Furthermore, when you swing with your body and racket you swing a large pendulum that has power. More power is generated when you swing from the legs and hips than when you swing from just the shoulder or elbow.

Note that you don't need to take a long swing to generate power. A short, compact swing, using your legs and good timing, creates lots of power.

Of course you don't always need power. On many shots you need quick reactions more than power. If you swing your whole body at a net volley, the ball is likely to be past you before your racket can hit it. You need both power shots and quick reaction shots. You need to know which pendulum— which hitting system—to use.

An Array of Pendulums is Available to You

A small pendulum swings faster than a large pendulum. Your body has many different pendulums to use. Once you understand timing, your body will naturally swing with the right hitting system for the shot you're making.

The backswing/forward swing sequence needs to be a lot quicker and shorter when you hit a rushed volley than when you hit a smooth groundstroke. You'll also need to swing quickly when you hit a half-volley, a ball that lands unexpectedly near your feet. Both shots require you to swing a smaller hitting mass than would a groundstroke in the backcourt where you have time to set up for your hit.

If you swing just your forearm and racket you'll be hitting with a relatively short, light pendulum that can be swung quickly for these quick reaction shots.

For normal groundstrokes—those in the backcourt— swinging your whole body and arm is better. That means you'll swing more slowly, but in the backcourt there is time to execute this more powerful swing.

Now don't get confused. All your swings should be compact. But on groundstrokes the compact swing includes your hips and shoulders. On volleys the compact swing includes just your forearm and racket. *No* swing should be made by bringing the hitting arm way back behind you.

Exploring Timing

First, Just the Racket

Find somewhere that you and your tennis racket can be

alone, where you can concentrate. Your living room would be fine. I want you to swing different hitting systems to get the feel of each. Keep the clock pendulum in mind and try to swing as freely as the clock pendulum.

For the first drill, hold a racket with your hitting hand, letting it hang comfortably downward. Tuck your hitting elbow next to your body to keep your elbow from moving and let the racket swing back and forth in your hand. Keep your forearm still. Hold the racket loosely in your fingers so your wrist is free to move. Let the racket swing from the wrist and try not to force it. Get the feeling of this wristy swing. (Swinging with your wrist is *not* the way to swing a tennis racket in play; it is being employed here strictly as an instructional technique.)

Next swing your forearm and racket from your elbow, keeping the wrist straight. Again, swing as effortlessly as possible and feel the timing of this swing. Grip the racket very loosely. A tight grip prevents a free swing. Note that when you swing from the elbow the natural swing is slower than when you swing from the wrist. That's because you're using a larger pendulum.

Now extend your arm comfortably so your elbow is a few inches from your side, and swing your whole arm and racket as a unit from your shoulder. This time keep the wrist *and* elbow from bending. Let the swing occur, don't force it. Again, maintain a gentle grip. If you are doing this effortlessly, the swing rhythm should again be much slower.

Next, swing your whole body, arm and racket as one large hitting system, swinging from the hips and using your legs to help. Swing your whole body smoothly by turning your torso from side to side. Try to keep your wrist, elbow and shoulder fixed as you swing this way. Note that turning the torso makes the racket go back and forth without bringing your arm back. The torso turn brings the racket back.

To reiterate, when you swing from the wrist, your swing is short and fast. As you swing from the elbow, and then the shoulder, the swing becomes slower and longer. When you swing your whole body, the overall swing is longer and slower still.

Swing these different hitting systems until you can swing each one, effortlessly. Take plenty of time to try this, and do it often. Think about the clock's pendulum and try to swing whichever hitting system you're testing as smoothly as a pendulum. Being able to do this exercise is essential. You won't feel timing on the court if you can't feel it when you swing off the court.

Swing fully, as though you were hitting a real ball. Don't baby your practice swings. Focus on the rhythm of each swing, and see how little effort is needed when you allow the swing to occur at its own speed. Try swinging too fast; observe how much energy and muscle power is involved and how unnatural it feels. Your goal is to swing as effortlessly on the court as you do in your living room.

On to the Backboard

Once you get the feeling of good timing without hitting a ball, find a backboard. Then experiment again with effortless swings as you hit a ball against the backboard. Don't hit hard, hit smoothly. (A suggestion for backboard practice: Let the ball bounce twice before you hit it; this will give you more time between hits and create conditions more closely resembling actual play.)

Do a lot of this backboard hitting. It will allow you to concentrate on and get the feeling of good timing. Try different hitting systems on the backboard. Try hitting with just the forearm and racket, as you would on volleys or half-volleys. Hit with your whole body, as you would on groundstrokes.

And Finally to the Court

Then try it all on the court with a practice partner. Hit smoothly. Experiment with swinging until you understand the perfect rhythm of your swing timing. Again, keep the clock pendulum in mind as you practice. See how efficiently you can swing—how power can be generated without effort. Become very *aware* of timing; focus on it. Explore what it is.

Good timing will become part of your game through this kind of awareness and exploration.

When to Start the Swing

Timing and Newton

Good timing involves not only swinging your racket but also knowing when to start your swing. The swinging pendulum analogy helped us understand what a smooth swing should feel like. But pendulums swing back and forth continuously. Your tennis swing doesn't. It starts with your racket held stationary in front of you, not swinging. When do you start to swing?

Recall Newton's Law of Motion: For every action there is an equal and opposite reaction. To roll a bowling ball down the alley, you first swing it back behind you, then swing it forward and then let it go. To turn a bicycle to the right, you must first turn slightly to the left so you can lean right to turn that way. In both these movements there is no delay between the action and reaction. The action causes the reaction. A delay would interfere with the smoothness of the sequence.

In tennis, you swing the racket back so you can swing it forward, neither rushing or nor delaying. That's action and reaction at work. Because the racket is light, you can use your muscles to do almost anything you want with it. The flip side is that your muscles can also disrupt the timing of the backswing/ forward swing sequence. If you bring your racket back too early, you end up delaying the forward swing while you wait for the ball. If you react late to the ball you compensate by pulling the racket back suddenly and then forcing it forward. The result is poor timing and a poorly hit ball.

Why You Can't Get Tennis Elbow From Bowling

You wouldn't and couldn't do that with the bowling ball. The ball is too heavy. You swing it back and let it swing forward when it's ready. If you don't—if you delay it at the back of your swing, or if you jerk it back too fast—you'll hurt your shoulder.

In tennis, however, it's easy to commit errors in timing without immediately realizing it and without immediately hurting yourself. This can produce two unfortunate consequences: your game suffers and *you risk developing tennis elbow over a prolonged period of improper hitting.*

If the racket is to meet the ball at the right time, then the forward swing must react naturally to the backswing as Newton says. It should follow the backswing without delay. That, in turn, means the backswing must start at the right time— not too late, nor too early.

Repeat the backswing/forward swing sequence until you naturally start your swing at the right time. Feel how the forward swing can be a natural reaction to the backswing once the backswing is started.

Practice the action/reaction sequence at home. Hold the racket in front of you and imagine a ball coming at you. Bring the racket back and then swing it forward to meet the mental ball with natural swing timing. Do this by swinging from the wrist, the elbow, the shoulder, and then with the whole body.

Once you feel proper timing, it will seem awkward to swing without it. You will have made a breakthrough.

Timing and Your Wrist

Swing So Your Wrist Stays Fixed

Nothing in tennis is more damaging to your game (and irritating) than having your wrist flip as you meet the ball with your racket. The ball loses speed and power and flies off in the wrong direction.

It's all right to turn or break your wrist when you play ping-pong. The ball is light, the distance involved is small and getting the ball where and how you want it can be accomplished literally with the flick of a wrist. By and large that doesn't work with tennis. On rare occasions—such as when they're at the net and must react instantly—good players with the necessary strength and control will meet the ball by flicking the racket with their wrists. But even tournament players do not practice such wristy shots because they don't want to get in the habit of hitting that way.

Instructors emphasize swinging so that your wrist stays fixed. Good players know that wrist movement costs power and control.

Your wrist will automatically stay fixed if you are balanced, swing with proper timing and meet the ball well in front of you. One reason that hitting out in front is so important is that it allows you to keep your wrist fixed.

The accompanying illustrations show the fixed-wrist swing from start to finish. Note the wrist is fixed in the cocked-open position and stays that way throughout the swing. That's consistent with hitting the ball out in front. Note also that the ball is met well in front of the hitter. The middle picture shows the impact point in front of the hitter.

Beware of the Difference Between Cause and Effect

Consider the following two statements:

• Swing so your wrist stays fixed.
• Keep your wrist fixed when you swing.

Do they mean the same thing to you? They better not if you want to play decent tennis.

The first statement is telling us that if you swing properly the wrist will remain fixed. It's a sound insight.

The second statement is not. In fact, it is terrible advice. Contrary to what it implicitly promises, keeping the wrist fixed will *not* cause a good swing.

A well-timed swing with the ball met in front of the body leads to a properly fixed wrist. Keeping your wrist fixed does not necessarily lead to good timing.

Hitting late causes a wristy swing. The wrist compensates for lateness by forcing the racket through quickly. If you're late, it's easier to force just the racket—that is, to "wrist" it—than to force your arm *and* racket. Because the racket weighs less than arm plus racket, it can be moved more quickly. Therefore being late causes wristiness. Learn to swing so you're not late.

Shadow Hitting

To develop a perfectly timed fixed-wrist stroke, practice swinging your arm without holding a racket. Pretend your palm is the racket, and that you're hitting an imaginary ball with your palm. Let the imaginary impact point occur in front of your

torso. Swing freely, like a pendulum.

Swing several dozen times, but each time you swing, swing your arm so as to hit *through* the imaginary ball with your palm. Pretend your palm determines which way the ball will go. Hitting through the ball means accelerating through the impact point—increasing your hand speed even after the impact point.

As you swing your arm, pay close attention to your wrist. If you swing like a pendulum, meet the imaginary ball in front of you and accelerate your hand as you hit, then your wrist should remain fixed—and cocked open—throughout the swing.

Now Swing a Racket Without a Ball

Once you get the feeling of a well-timed, fixed-wrist swing with just your arm, try swinging with the racket.

Again, swing at imaginary balls. But now think of the racket hitting the ball *with your palm leading the racket*. Hit as though you want the handle to lead the racket head through the entire swing. Accelerate your hitting system—arm, hand and racket—through the imaginary impact point, with the racket

Keep a fixed wrist. The wrist is in the correct position at ball impact and remains "fixed" throughout the entire swing. Position and timing are adjusted so the wrist naturally stays fixed without being forced to do so.

trailing your hand. Keep swinging smoothly, like a pendulum, as you do this.

Your wrist should remain as fixed as it was when you were swinging without a racket.

Do a lot of this imaginary swinging. You can do it at home with your racket, for example, while watching television, or with your fold-up umbrella while walking to work.

It's important to swing perfectly without hitting a ball, until it's natural to do so without your wrist breaking even the least bit.

Then you're likely to swing through the real ball the same way—with your wrist naturally staying fixed.

A Worthwhile Tip: "Butt First"

I know I've told you I'm against tips. But "pull the racket through the ball butt first" is one tip that seems to work. That's because it focuses on an action. It keeps your mind on both the racket *and* the ball. The previous illustration shows the butt of the racket handle pointing at the ball on the backswing. That's what I mean by "butt first."

When you swing properly you should feel your hand pulling the racket, handle first, so that the racket head actually trails behind your hand as you swing. That helps you hit with your wrist fixed, and allows you to accelerate through the ball.

Most people find it helps to think "pull the butt end of the racket through the ball." By that I mean to think of pointing the butt end of your racket at the approaching ball as you start to swing forward, and then pull the racket straight through the swing, almost as though you were going to hit the ball with the butt end of the racket handle. (Don't worry, the racket head, not the handle, will hit the ball.) It works on groundstrokes, on volleys, and even overheads.

One student told me that "butt first" didn't make sense to her. So I suggested she think of hitting the ball with her palm or hitting handle first, or hitting with her hand pulling the racket, or "hand first, racket head last." One of these clicked, and she soon started pulling the racket through the ball without using her wrist. You may need to experiment with the words until they make sense to you.

Pulling the racket "butt first" (or handle first or palm first) means the racket need not be gripped tightly, but instead can be held gently. So besides improving your swing, "butt first" saves energy.

The Keys to Good Timing

First, it's important to practice swinging like a pendulum so that the feeling becomes part of you.

Second, it's important that your timing incorporates good action and reaction, so that when you hit an actual ball you will start your swing at the right time.

Third, be aware of your balance as you swing. Become balanced. (More on this in the next chapter.)

Fourth, develop your timing and balance within the basic mechanics of a compact swing, moving into the ball, meeting it in front of you, driving through it, and making the ball rise upward so it clears the net safely.

Finally, do not work on your timing during a match. Work on it during practice, so that it becomes part of your muscle memory. When you're playing to win, concentrate on the mental game: react to the ball and make your racket hit through the impact point.

11

Balance Is More Than Not Falling

BALANCE IS ABOUT THE WAY YOU MOVE BEFORE, DURING AND after the swing. Balance and timing are interrelated. Swinging with poor timing throws you off balance. Poor balance disrupts your timing.

The results of being balanced are obvious. When you're balanced you set up so you can step into the ball, using your whole body to generate power. Your timing is better because the swing flows more naturally, and you can swing more fully when you're balanced. If you're balanced *as* you swing you're more likely to be balanced when you finish the swing, which means you'll be in a position to react better on your next shot. It's easier, for example, to change directions when you're balanced.

Being balanced is more than merely not falling over. A person able to stand on one leg is balanced, but that's not balance for our purposes. He lacks stability and quickness. Balance in tennis means you're balanced all the time, when standing, moving and hitting.

When you are balanced you achieve two important benefits. The first is a sense of stability—meaning that if you are balanced a slight push would not throw you off balance. Second is potential quickness. You react faster when you're balanced on both feet, ready to move in any direction. Balancing on one leg gives you neither stability nor quickness.

Being out of balance slows your reaction time. The next time you play, instead of reminding yourself to be *ready* when your opponent hits, try telling yourself to be *balanced*. That will make you ready.

Balance and Power

Hitting with your body produces much more power than hitting just with your arms because the mass being used to hit with is greater.

When you're balanced you can hit with your body. When you're not, you tend to hit just with your arms. You usually can get the ball over the net but not with anything like the kind of power you're capable of.

But to get your body into the shot, you need to be balanced as you begin to swing.

If you learn to hit with your body, you'll not only be more balanced, but you'll react faster to surprise shots such as volleys. That's because moving from a balanced position is quicker.

Balance and Individual Parts of the Body

Balance applies to your whole body—but also to parts of it. You need your body balanced as you move around the court, keeping your weight more or less balanced between your feet. But you also need to keep your arms, your head, and your racket balanced as you play.

If you are too close to the ball when you hit you'll be off-balance, and swing with a cramped, powerless swing. Or you may be stretching your arm too far to hit. Your arms have a lot to do with balance. Be conscious of them.

How do you know when you're using your arms correctly? Find out where they are most comfortable when you swing. It doesn't matter whether you're hitting a groundstroke, an overhead or a volley. The point at which your arms are most comfortable is where they will be balanced.

Exploring Balance

The way to improve balance in your tennis is the way you improve other areas of your game. Explore it until you get it right.

To reach a point where you are almost always balanced while you play tennis—and reap the rewards that I've mentioned—you are going to have to explore balance fully. This may sound odd. You've spent your life being balanced; you're balanced all day long. It doesn't seem like something you need to master. You've already mastered it. Even if you acknowledge that balance is important, you probably are not inclined to spend time on it as you practice.

Believe me, it's worth the time.

Charlene Explores Her Balance

Charlene was an advanced player, already ranked among the top 20 women in her region. But she double-faulted too often, and that cost her matches. One night after playing mixed doubles she asked me if I saw anything wrong with her serve. I had noticed she seemed to twist sideways after meeting the ball instead of naturally falling forward toward the court. I asked her if she had ever thought about her balance.

"What do you mean?"

"See if you're balanced when you hit the serve."

I told her what being balanced felt like for me when I served well. I was balanced before the toss, during the swing, and as I landed on the court after the hit. I'd drive straight up through the ball instead of bending sideways as I swung. Even the ball toss was made smoothly, so it didn't throw me off balance.

I showed her by serving a few balls being balanced, and then a few more being deliberately off-balance. I suggested she explore balance the next time she practiced, and see if it made any difference.

It was late, and the whole discussion took only five minutes, but she seemed to understand what she might try.

Two weeks later Charlene won a state tournament in the women's open division. The next time I saw her she said I'd cured her serve. "The balance thing did it," she said.

I asked what she'd done, and she replied she just practiced being balanced—on her toss, her swing, and her step into the court.

Charlene did not learn about balance in those two weeks, she already had balance. All she did was become *aware* of it as she served, and the awareness made balance show up in her game.

Just Be Aware of Balance

You don't need to be taught balance. There are no steps to follow or mechanics to employ. In tennis, because of the moving you do, it's easy to get out of balance. To make sure you're balanced, all you need to do is to become conscious of being balanced, to become aware of it. When you hit a serve, simply seek the feeling of balance. As you see a ball coming toward you in practice, ask yourself if you are balanced as you hit or if you could be more balanced than you are.

It's amazing how much it helps your play just to be aware of balance.

Explore by Watching Yourself and Others

Work to become perfectly balanced *as you swing*. Be balanced at impact. Look for the following symptoms of imbalance: hitting late; forcing or muscling the racket through the ball; adjusting your body to compensate for being out of position; inability to recover smoothly.

Watch other people play. A pro will be balanced as he or she hits, but balance isn't as obvious as imbalance. Watch a tennis pro and then watch some intermediates on a nearby court. Keep comparing the difference. Try to visualize how you play to see if there are things you do that are more like the intermediate than the advanced player.

Balance and Parts of the Game

Footwork

Being balanced means moving your feet to stay balanced. It means bouncing, hopping, shuffling, running, leaping. There is much to be said of footwork. Still, *working* on footwork is not the best way to improve your footwork.

That sounds contradictory. But your footwork's muscle memory has been a lifetime developing. It won't change easily. Your tennis is more likely to adjust to your footwork than the other way around.

The way to better footwork is to work on balance, not footwork. Your footwork will improve if you get balanced. The opposite is not true. Work on your footwork, and your balance may well get worse, especially if you try to learn other people's footwork. They didn't learn to jump and run the way you jump and run.

It's another example of how we get cause and effect backward. Good footwork results because you stay balanced, not the other way around. If you were losing your balance and about to fall off a cliff, you would not be concentrating on how to move your feet. You'd be concentrating on keeping your balance—really focusing on balance—and your feet would move accordingly. That's the kind of focus on balance I'm asking you to be aware of when practicing tennis.

Hitting Hard

Most of us would like to hit hard. But we also realize there's such a thing as trying to hit too hard. When that happens shots go awry.

I suggest you always hit as hard as you can while still being in balance. Swinging so hard you're not balanced means you are swinging too hard.

If you keep your mind focused on the hitting action—making the racket meet the ball—you'll quickly become aware of how hard you can swing and still be balanced. Experiment with hitting hard. See if you can detect a point at which your swing becomes too forceful to stay balanced. More likely than not, you'll find you can swing much harder than you thought.

Balance and Hitting Out in Front

When you're balanced, you'll hit the ball with your hitting hand well in front of you. If you meet the ball with your hitting hand near your side you'll be unbalanced.

To see why, experiment with your elbows. When standing with your elbows slightly in front of your hips, it's easier to be balanced than when they are too far behind your hips. If your elbows are slightly in front of your hips, then your hands will be well in front of your body. Hit with your hands out in front of you like that. It will help keep you balanced.

Going After Lobs

When a lob is hit over your head in doubles, you should not try for it just because you can reach it. You should only go for it if you can hit it in balance. If you can't, it's better to yell "Yours" and let your partner get it. If you are the partner, be ready to cover overheads that will be too deep for your partner to reach easily. Too many of us try to hit every overhead we can stretch for, and wind up missing the ball, making weak returns or falling.

This applies to singles too. Older players, and those not completely comfortable with the acrobatics of overheads, should take care not to hit overheads too far out of balance. Bad falls can occur. Better to run back, letting the ball bounce, and hit a defensive lob in return.

Overheads

As you await a lob that you are fully capable of hitting with an overhead, check whether your hitting arm is in balance. It should be poised above you *comfortably* so you can hit upward through the ball in balance. If your arm is held in an arbitrary backscratch position—as is usually recommended—you will not feel comfortable or balanced. And letting your arm hang by your side while your opponent's lob approaches you will not allow you to be ready to hit.

Overheads should feel comfortable. Both arms should be comfortably held up above your shoulders as you get into position to hit. Your head should be balanced between your shoulders as you hit and should not need to compensate for imbalance as you complete the shot. Watch intermediate players and see how often they hit overheads out of balance: upper bodies twisted, heads cocked awkwardly to one side.

Serving

When you throw the tennis ball up to serve, your tossing arm should move gracefully. A jerky toss that pulls you off balance will make your serve erratic.

Volleying

Keep your racket balanced with the racket head more or less upright as you approach the net for a volley. If the racket hangs from your hand, pointing toward the court, it will take longer for you to react than if it's balanced in your hand, ready to be punched through the volley.

12

Timing Plus Balance Equal Strokes

TENNIS IS A SPORT OF STROKES. BALANCE AND TIMING DETERmine the quality of your strokes. You improve your strokes as well as the rest of your physical game by practicing balance and timing as you hit different strokes.

I reluctantly discuss strokes; it automatically means introducing some mechanics into tennis, something I'm usually opposed to. I do so here because I have found that you gain insight into balance and timing as you see how they affect the efficiency of your strokes.

We all stroke differently, so it is impossible to provide detailed descriptions of each stroke. There are, however, general insights that apply to each stroke and are worth considering. Try to gain the insights without becoming too concerned about the mechanics.

The Forehand

There's the normal forehand, the one you use to hit balls that are easy to get to and allow you plenty of time to set up properly. A more difficult forehand is the one you have to hit on the run.

As the ball approaches your forehand, react quickly to intercept it. Start your backswing while you're running, so you will be able to swing smoothly and without delay. But make sure it's part of the continuous pendulum swing. Do not bring the racket back early to hold it in anticipation of the stroke. If you have the time, come to a stop so that you can take a step into the ball as you hit. But odds are you won't have the time.

Be *aware* of the possibility of overrunning the ball. If you get too close to it you'll be forced into using a cramped, powerless swing. The result will be a ball with little zip. Simply being aware of the possibility may be enough to avoid it.

You will find it easier to produce a compact swing if you turn your shoulders to start the swing. The shoulder turn brings your racket back; then, in one powerful motion, you step forward and swing through the ball. You need to experiment with that sequence to see if you can do it in balance with perfect timing.

To help keep the swing compact, don't bring the racket back too far. Keep your hitting elbow near your hipbone if you can.

If all that sounds too mechanical, try this to get the feeling of a good forehand. Think again about throwing that 10-pound bag of potatoes into the back of the pickup truck. You hold the bag in both hands, turn your shoulders and hips to bring it back a little, then step forward and heave the bag, unwinding your coiled body and driving with your legs. Note that you would not bring the bag of potatoes behind you to throw it. You'd hold it in front of you and use your body and legs for forward power. Do the same with a tennis racket when hitting a forehand.

One-handed Backhands

You do very few things in day-to-day life resembling the motion of a one-handed backhand. It requires you to cross your hitting hand over to the opposite side of your body and then swing it forward, with the back of the hand leading. It's an awkward motion. It's not at all like throwing a bag of potatoes. It's like throwing a frisbee, which may give you a sense of how a backhand should feel.

Many people find frisbee-throwing awkward at first but easy after some practice. The same can be true of one-handed backhands.

Ironically, the inherent awkwardness makes most one-handed backhands well-timed. You are forced to hit with good timing, because the backhand muscles are not well developed. The muscles are underdeveloped precisely because you do so few things that are like the one-handed backhand. Even strong men are compelled to use good timing to hit one-handed backhands, as there is little muscle available to force the shot.

Because it's a stroke hit with the weaker side of your arm, the one-handed backhand needs to be started with a somewhat longer backswing to generate power. This can be seen in the accompanying illustration. It's almost impossible to hit an effective one-handed backhand while employing a swing as compact as the two-handed backhand or the forehand. The reduced muscle power makes it difficult to move your arms and body as a unit the way you can on those shots. Thus, the one-handed backhand calls for a longer, smoother swing.

Most players, however, tend to bring the racket too far back on the one-hander and as a result hit late. It's better to shorten the swing a little, and then meet the ball well out in front of you. The hitting hand can be brought back to about the thigh on the backswing.

Be sure to pull the racket all the way through the ball. Experiment with pulling the butt end of the racket handle through the ball, with the racket head trailing your hitting hand, to get the right feeling.

Most important, *feel* smoothness and comfort in your swing. If the swing feels awkward, explore swinging like a pendulum until the timing seems right. You can do that between points and at home. Hit lots of imaginary balls that way.

If after all this the one-handed backhand still feels weak or awkward, consider changing to a two-hander. (If you're going to make the switch through lessons, make sure to find a pro who naturally hits with a two-handed backhand. Don't go to a pro who hits one-handed; he or she won't know the true feeling of the two-hander.)

The Two-handed Backhand

The two-handed backhand offers some advantages over the more traditional one-handed variety. It is powerful because the body automatically becomes part of the hitting system. In fact, it's awkward to swing the racket using two hands without swinging the body as well.

Using the body means the hitting system has considerable mass, and with good timing that generates power. The two-hander also speeds reaction time because the racket can be swung compactly and quickly.

But there is a downside to the two-handed backhand: using it can lead to poor timing. Because both arms are employed, there is plenty of muscle power available to compensate for lateness. There is the danger that a player using a two-handed backhand will muscle the ball over the net instead of relying on good timing in his stroke. If you watch intermediates who use two-handed backhands you'll notice that they often hit late and swing too quickly.

Usually lateness produces wristiness. With a two-handed backhand it normally doesn't, simply because it is hard to wrist a swing when using two hands. Instead, lateness is compensated for by the body stepping backward away from the approaching ball rather than into it—which is why you will often see late-swinging two-handed players fall away from a shot, losing power.

When exploring timing on your two-handed backhand, observe whether your body weight is moving forward as you hit. If it is moving backwards, you have an opportunity to improve your backhand and its power. Be aware of your balance at impact. If you are not moving into the ball as you hit, you'll need to keep at this until the action of stepping into the ball is stored in your muscle memory.

Think once again of tossing a bag of potatoes, but do it from the backhand side to get a feeling for the two-handed backhand.

For someone who is right-handed, the two-handed backhand should be swung with the left hand providing the power while the right hand merely guides the racket. Using the right hand for power will cause the racket to be pulled across the ball, costing both power and accuracy.

A well-executed two-handed backswing will have your feet spread and your weight balanced mostly on the left foot (for right-handers) on the backswing. The backswing is accomplished by a hip and shoulder turn, so that on the backswing your hands are in front of you, no further back than your hipbone.

The proper forward swing will feel like the body uncoils to lead the arms, and the arms lead the hands through the impact point. Recall the tip to pull the racket handle "butt first" through the ball. That works as well on the two-handed backhand as it does on the forehand. Be sure to meet the ball well out in front so that when you pull through the ball you do not need to flick your wrists. Keep the wrists in the same position throughout the swing. They should be cocked open. The illustrations that follow show the fixed-wrist position.

Volleys

The volley is difficult for many players because of the need to react so quickly. Consequently, a volley is usually hit with only the forearm and racket; there is seldom time to bring into play such other parts of your hitting system as your shoulders and torso.

But before you reach the point of physically executing

Backhands. For the one-handed backhand the racket is brought further back than for the two-hander, but not so far back as to throw the hitter off balance.

The one-hander is more naturally hit with a closed stance, with the hitter sideways to the net. The two-handed backhand can be hit facing the net. This provides both power and deception. Note how the wrist stays fixed throughout both sequences.

the stroke, you must react successfully, and that process starts with the mind, not the body. Begin by mentally focusing on the approaching ball and making your racket meet it. That's more important than anything else you can do.

Most people who have trouble volleying will improve fastest by trying to block the ball rather than trying to hit it. Blocking the ball means putting your racket up and letting the ball bounce off the racket. That's the right action at first. Once you are able to block the ball consistently, you can begin to try for more power by hitting *through* the volley.

You can shorten your reaction time by holding your racket in front of you and being light on your feet. Use this stance when you're practicing at the net so that it becomes part of your muscle memory.

Late, wristy shots are common on volleys; it is easy to be late when a hard shot is hit at you. Avoid wristiness by keeping your hitting hand in front of you and blocking the ball. More advanced players can *pull* the racket through the ball. Pulling the racket through the ball with the wrist firm will produce the underspin on volleys that you want.

Practice timing your volley by focusing on turning your shoulders so that you can meet the ball in front of your chest and still hit the ball in the direction you choose. Keep your racket hand well in front of you throughout the hit, particularly on the one-handed backhand. A late one-handed backhand volley is very weak and quickly results in tennis elbow. Volleys *must* be hit well out in front of you—that is, in front of your torso.

Use your legs to get forward motion into your volleys. Don't rely on a normal backswing/forward swing motion. Hold your racket in front of you when at the net waiting for your opponent's hit. Be balanced. A good volleyer will step forward as the ball approaches, put the racket up to intercept the ball and then pull the racket through the ball. Very little or no racket swing is needed. Think of driving the racket strings through the impact point with your hand leading the racket face. That will keep your wrist firm. Work on the timing of this until your wrist *naturally* stays fixed throughout the hit.

It's important to practice hitting volleys with your attention focused on balance and timing as you hit. The volley should feel relaxed and comfortable. At first, don't worry about where your balls go. They may hit the net or even the back fence for a while. Let them. Keep your mind on balance and timing. It will help if your practice partner has a basket of 50 or so balls to hit to you. Or use a backboard, hitting gentle half-volleys—balls that you hit on the rise just after they bounce—until you get a feel for the quick-reaction timing needed for full volleys.

Eventually, your volleys will become controlled. They will require less and less motion. A good volleyer pulls the racket through the ball, hitting slightly under the ball to cause underspin (also known as backspin).

Experiment with pulling the racket butt through the ball. It works on volleys as well as groundstrokes. Hitting slightly under the ball gives it backspin and also makes it rise as it leaves your racket face. That will make the volley go deeper. If you focus on meeting the ball well out in front of you, the ball will not fly off the court.

Become aware of how your volley *feels* as you hit. Be aware of the feel of the very short racket swing, the feeling of the impact, and the feeling of the racket in your hand after impact. The hand should still lead the racket. That will happen if you swing so that your wrist naturally stays fixed.

Become aware of whether the entire sequence is effortless or labored. It should be effortless. Note whether the racket feels balanced in your hand as you hit. Observe any wristy lateness. Be prepared for some frustration at first and do not treat early lack of success as failure.

Half-volleys and Approach Shots

Half-volleys are those reactive shots you employ to handle balls that bounce at your feet, often catching you in mid-court and leaving you with little time to swing. Essentially, a half-volley is hit with the same timing as volleys. They usually require more loft to clear the net since your racket often meets them near your feet. That means you need to get down low to hit them, or else scoop under them with your racket when there's no time to bend.

Approach shots are slightly different, primarily because there is more time to hit them. An approach shot is a short ball that you attack and drive deeply into your opponent's court. Since you are meeting the ball as you approach the net, naturally you will be moving forward. Often the forward motion involves several running steps before you meet the ball. This

---

Volleying: It's Mental, Not Physical

Volleying can be difficult. Standing at the net facing a speeding ball can be intimidating. Executing the moves and strokes necessary to return that speeding ball can leave you, especially as a beginner, feeling uncoordinated.

What helps—particularly for beginners and for intermediates who don't like to come to the net—is to forget that volleying is a physical act and concentrate only on the thought of the racket meeting the ball.

Specifically, focus on the fact that the ball will come and that the racket should meet it. Don't think about how that is done.

Forget about hitting out front, the compact swing, hitting through the ball, employing a firm wrist and all the other components that make up a good swing. Just focus on somehow making the racket meet the ball.

If you're having real problems getting the knack of volleying, try something slightly different. Try simply getting the racket up into the path of the ball and letting the ball bounce off the racket. Don't try to hit the ball, let the ball hit the racket. But tilt your racket slightly so the ball bounces off it and rises upward to clear the net.

---

means you will be trying to swing your racket forward *as* you run. Your forward momentum will make it difficult to swing your racket to meet the ball out in front unless you run with the racket held in front of you. Your body movement provides enough power for the shot, so your swing can be minimal. The resulting action is similar to an unrushed volley or half-volley.

Punch through the ball as you would a volley, using little or no backswing.

Meet the ball well in front of you.

Hitting "butt first" will help.

Do not try to stop before you hit. That common advice is misleading because you will seldom have time to stop and start again. So be prepared to hit on the run, but do make sure you are balanced and that your timing is good. Practicing balance and timing on approach shots will be far more useful than working on footwork, the usual advice. A good three-person drill for practicing approach shots is discussed in Chapter 16.

Serves and Overheads

Serves and overheads are met above your head. Hitting above your head is awkward. It tends to throw you off balance, so exploring balance is particularly useful in those shots. Timing is more natural on serves and overheads because both allow more response time than other shots. The serve is completely controlled by the server, and overheads hang in the air for a while, usually allowing adequate time to swing. Being balanced while your chin points skyward, however, is not so natural.

As with other shots, hit *through* the ball on serves and overheads. Keep accelerating the hitting hand through the impact point. The wrist should not break before the ball is hit—try to swing the racket "butt first" when you practice, and see if that helps you generate power and accuracy. Try to pull the racket handle up through the ball to get the feeling of acceleration through the ball.

Also incorporate into the stroke the upward drive of your legs. It will provide power. This upward drive makes the ball clear the net safely. Most service faults and overhead errors are balls hit into the net rather than balls hit long.

It may seem surprising that overheads should be hit with the racket moving *upward* through the ball instead of downward, to put away the shot. The ball must be hit upward because you want it to clear the net comfortably, go deep into your opponent's court and yet land inside the baseline. To accomplish all that requires topspin, and the way to generate topspin is to hit up on the back of the ball.

The wrist will break after ball impact—it is practically impossible to prevent that—but more power is generated if the wrist is held back as long as possible. The power results from the wrist snap occurring as the ball leaves the racket, rather than before or at impact. But if you try to *make* the wrist snap—instead of simply *letting* it snap—much of the momentum of the body and arm is lost. That is why I'm down on the tip "snap the wrist through the serve." It causes inconsistency.

Serves and overheads should be feel like you're throwing a javelin or a spear. Javelins are thrown upward, toward the sky, and so are good serves and overheads.

The Service Toss

The serve has one overlooked aspect of timing—the toss. Your tossing arm should be swung upward with its own natural timing. Many players jerk the tossing arm up too quickly, denying its natural swing rhythm. Analogous to the backswing/forward swing sequence, the toss requires lowering, then raising, the arm. This should be done smoothly and comfortably.

You often hear professionals say the toss is the most important part of the serve. Experiment with perfect timing on your service toss, and you will find that your toss becomes error-free. Your serve will benefit from that. And if your serve is on, the rest of your game can be played with more confidence.

PART FOUR

SOME FURTHER THOUGHTS ABOUT TENNIS

WHAT FOLLOWS ARE THOUGHTS ON TENNIS that can contribute significantly to breakthroughs, but which do not fall exclusively or easily into the previous sections on learning and the mental and physical games. Necessarily there is some overlap but it is minimal and, like most elements of sound tennis information, worth going over again.

13

What to Do With Your Hands and Feet

IN TENNIS THERE ARE THINGS YOU DO WITH YOUR HANDS besides swinging a racket. You use your hands to determine *how* and *where* you position the racket and *when* you swing it. This can be as important as the stroke itself.

Similarly, what you do with your feet determines where you are when you hit the ball—in the right spot or in the wrong spot. Active footwork will help you be balanced, and you know how critical balance is to reacting and swinging well.

Moving your feet even has something to do with your morale on court. A player who bounces lightly on his toes while awaiting the ball is psychologically ready for successful play. Conversely, nine times out of ten a tennis player who is down on himself, who is dejected and lacking in confidence, is flat-footed, slow to react and careless in his strokes.

Running in to Hit

Nothing is more frustrating in tennis than rushing in for a short ball and then missing a seemingly easy put-away shot. Don't be so hard on yourself. Swinging a racket when you're running forward is very different from swinging a racket when you're standing still. Those "easy" shots are not all that easy.

The Physics of Running Forward

When you are in the backcourt hitting a ball—that is, *not* running in—you might swing the racket at 75 miles an hour. When you're running toward the net at 15 mph, the racket would need to move at 90 mph—its normal 75 mph plus your 15 in order to keep pace with your body's movement.

That's why you tend to hit the ball badly when you run in toward the net. You hit late. You do so because you can't get the racket through to the ball as easily as when you're not moving.

Ninety percent of your shots are hit while *not* running forward. Your timing gets grooved—comes to respond automatically—to that kind of shot. Then, when your opponent hits a short ball, you rush in to put it away—and hit it long or into the net. You berate yourself for missing a put-away shot.

How to Hit Successfully While Running

Most tennis pros will tell you that if you're running in for a ball, come to a stop before hitting. It eliminates the problem of coordinating your swing with your moving body. But stopping is not always practical. If you're running in, you're doing it to get to the ball, sometimes just barely reaching it in time. You seldom have time to stop.

Nor need you stop. A ball can be hit on the run and hit well. There are two ways that I know of. The first is to shorten your backswing. That way the racket will stay further in front of you. You can swing and run at the same time and still get the racket to the impact point in front of you. The momentum of your body moving forward will more than make up for the shortened racket stroke. You won't lose power.

The second way is to choke up on your racket an inch or two. That will shorten the length of the pendulum you swing, therefore making it swing quicker. As it happens, this doesn't feel natural to me but a friend swears by it. We're all different.

I won't try to explain the ballistics of swinging your racket on the run. You need to experiment with these shots. But whatever you do, *remember to focus on the racket meeting the ball*. The danger with a put-away shot is the temptation to look—or even just to think of—where you're going to put it away. Either distraction can ruin the shot for you.

An Effective Hitting-and-running Drill

Mastery over the hit-and-run challenge can be achieved through practice. One useful drill goes like this: bounce a high, soft ball to yourself on a backboard, then run in and hit it on the run. These hits are not at all easy to control at first. But practice will give you the chance to explore hitting on the run.

Three crucial points to remember: The first is to concentrate on the racket meeting the ball. This has been said before in the context of hitting in general but needs to be continually re-emphasized. Second, meet the ball well out in front. Third, groove your swing so that your wrist is in the fixed-wrist position as you meet the ball.

Pulling the butt of the racket through the ball on these running-in shots helps. It keeps you from hitting late and prevents wristing the shot. The "butt-first" tip works.

Hands in Front for Volleying

When you volley, your hitting hand—whether forehand or backhand—should be in front of you. To get the right feeling, hold a glass of water comfortably in front of you. Now, without using any backswing, hit an imaginary forehand volley with the glass, trying not to spill any of the water.

Watch closely. You'll tip the glass forward *slightly* as you step into the shot to hit, and then tip it back as you swing. This down-up swoop (sort of in the shape of a banana) is the way your volleys should be hit. Contact is made on the upswing.

The backhand volley action—either one or two-handed—is the same. Try swinging the glass of water again to see the down-up swoop, and visualize hitting your backhand volley that way.

With only a little practice, you can swing the water glass quite rapidly without spilling any. The down-up swoop is the key, as it is on volleys.

Hitting down through the ball, without any upswing, may seem like the way to put away a ball but it isn't the right way to hit a volley. In the drill the water will spill out of the glass. On the tennis court, the ball will either hit the net or else bounce in such a way that your opponent will have a good crack at it. But if you hit with the racket rising slightly as you make impact, your ball will clear the net safely and land deep enough in the backcourt to make it difficult for your opponent to return effectively, giving you time to move early enough to attack the next shot.

Cutting Back on the Backswing

In tennis we're taught early on to "bring the racket back." As a result, we see beginners, as well as many intermediates, poised with their racket arms way back, awaiting the return.

Forget you ever heard it. At least for the moment. Instead of "bring the racket back," think to yourself, "get the hand forward."

Watch some of the hardest hitters among the pros. They don't bring their rackets back when they get into the ready position. The first thing they do is bounce a little to react to the ball. Then they turn their shoulders but instead of getting the racket back they get the hitting hand *out in front*. They don't bring the racket back *until they start the swing,* a few tenths of a second later, and even then, they don't bring the racket back very far. The backswing and the forward swing together make up a continuous pendulum swing. That usually isn't the case with those who bring the racket back.

The physics of the situation support what the pros do. Getting your hitting hand out in front, toward the approaching ball, allows you to be balanced as you start your swing.

Bringing the racket back as your first move, on the other hand, throws you *off*-balance. Try it. Stand and bring your arm back behind you. Odds are you won't be balanced.

Then try turning your shoulders sideways but keeping your hitting hand more or less out in front of you. That's more balanced. You can launch your attack on the ball from that position.

The harder the ball is coming at you, the more you should keep your hitting arm out in front of you. That's using a short backswing. When the ball is coming really fast it's better to use no backswing at all and attack the ball by driving forward with your legs, blocking the shot instead of swinging at it.

Try Using No Backswing

Practice hitting with no backswing at all. You will see the contribution your legs make toward achieving greater power and control in your strokes. This is because the only way to hit with no backswing is to hit with your legs.

Hold the racket in front of you as though it were already at the impact point and then try keeping it there while you hit a ball. To do so you'll need to move toward the ball, driving the racket through the impact point by using your legs to move your body and racket.

Many players find that hitting this way gives them added

control and more power. While you may not want to swing that way when you play, you'll find the exercise will encourage you during competition to move into the ball and to hit with a compact yet still powerful swing.

A Few Words About Footwork

You're pretty much stuck with the footwork you grew up with. At least when you're doing the things that you've done all your life, like running and jumping and turning. Try to run or turn differently, and you'll do it badly.

Still, while you're used to moving forward, you don't move sideways very often. Sideways moves, like reacting to volleys at the net and leaping for wide serves, are less ingrained. It can pay to work on the footwork involved in these by learning how to react.

Players who move around the court well are not always the fastest runners. They're the quickest "reacters." Reacting properly means being balanced and mentally alert as your opponent hits. It also means starting the right way. It means being ready to move your feet and that requires something like bouncing. Starting your move the right way means moving the correct foot first.

Bouncing

When I'm playing well, I bounce lightly as my opponent prepares to hit. When I'm not playing well, I don't bounce at all. I'm flat-footed, not on my toes. I'm slow to react and not ready.

Bouncing has a lot to do with balance. If you bounce, you'll tend to be balanced, light on your feet and quick.

Bouncing is not jumping. When you jump, you use your legs to lift your entire body weight off the ground. "Bouncing" means lifting your feet, not your body. When you bounce, your head doesn't move, but your feet, legs and buttocks do.

The thing to do is to explore bouncing, and see the different ways you can make your body weight ready to move quickly. You'll find the best way for *you* to be ready to move by doing that.

While bouncing gets you ready, your first reactive move is critical.

The Wrong Moves Can Be Costly

Many pros will tell you: When moving sideways to volley, cross one foot over the other. That's not good physics, and it costs you time.

It takes the average person half a second to begin to move—to go from being flat-footed to actually moving. It then takes just over another half-second to cross one foot over the other, that is to move to your right by crossing your left foot over, or vice versa.

On the other hand, it takes only a tenth of a second to lift the right foot and fall or lunge to the right. That means if you are ready and move properly, you will be in position to hit the tennis ball almost a full second sooner than someone who is flat-footed and begins the move improperly. One second is more than half the time you have to react to your opponent's shot. No wonder some people are rushed when they hit and others have plenty of time. Here's a good drill to help you make that first move a good one.

The Fly-kill Drill

Stand balanced, with your feet spread comfortably. Place a coin on the floor about two feet to your right and slightly in front of you. Now pretend the coin is a housefly you want to stomp on and kill.

How would you move to get the fly?

Get poised on the balls of your feet. To move quickly, take a lunging step with the right foot, the one nearest the fly. Lift

Quick reaction footwork.
The forehand volley (above) starts with the right foot stepping to the right. The backhand starts with the left foot stepping to the left.

Slow reaction footwork.
In the forehand volley sequence shown, the initial step to the right is taken by the left foot crossing over. This takes much more time than stepping to the right with the right foot as was done in the above sequence.

your right foot without shifting your weight, so that you fall to the right while you push off with your left foot. Catch yourself with the right foot as it lands on the target. This is not an easy thing to learn if it's not natural for you, but it can be learned. It can change you from being slow to being quick.

Try it. Be aware of how you can move the fastest. Crossing over—first taking a step with the left foot and then the right—is slow. It's no good shifting your weight to the left foot so you can step out with the right, either; that takes time, too.

Of course, you need to practice the drill to your left, too. Pick up the right foot when moving to the right, and the left when moving to the left.

Mostly you'll be told the opposite, to step over with the opposite foot to volley. That's not good physics. The crossover can be the *second* move, not the first. The accompanying figures should help.

Next time you're on the court, stand ready at the net with your feet apart and pretend to react to volleys to your right and left. Think about the fly-kill drill as you react. Do the same while standing at the base line, pretending your opponent hits hard serves to one side of you and the other. It will take some time to get over any awkwardness that comes from doing things differently.

14

So You Want to Play Power Tennis

IF YOU WANT TO HIT WITH POWER, TRY DOING WHAT MOST tennis instructors and most books say *not* to do.

They tell you *not* to face the net when you swing, that your side should be turned toward the net.

Violating a Cardinal Rule

I'm telling you that if you want to increase the power in your strokes, *try facing the net.* Or at least face the net partially. Keep your feet pointing more toward the net than toward the sideline. That's the way to hit with power.

Turning sideways takes time. It takes half a second to turn so that you're facing the sidelines. That's a half-second wasted in your reaction time.

What the Photographs Showed

In his 1962 book *Instant Tennis*, Dick Bradlee, a mechanical engineer, focused on the dynamics of the swing—specifically on how to use one's body to produce optimum power. Bradlee examined action photographs of such tennis greats as Lew Hoad, Budge Patty and Alice Marble and noticed something interesting. None of them turned sideways to hit with the traditionally taught closed stance. All of them stood facing the net when they met the ball.

Their feet faced the net while their shoulders turned sideways, coiling their bodies like springs ready to release the built-up tension.

In the classic sideways or closed stance, the feet point toward the sideline, and the body weight is fully transferred to the front foot before ball impact. Bradlee argued that tennis pros teach the classic closed stance, not realizing they themselves hit with wide-open stances.

Many years later I watched Andre Agassi—probably the hardest hitter on the tour at the time—and saw that he hit just the way Bradlee described. I applied the principle to my own playing and teaching.

Don's Story

Although tall and muscular, Don was hitting groundstrokes that lacked power. He told me he had been trying to do something about it by getting sideways to the net in order to swing more fully at the ball. I watched and saw he was indeed getting sideways, but instead of loosening up, his swing seemed cramped.

I asked him to forget everything he knew about hitting and simply hit the ball as hard as he could—that it was even okay if it went over the fence. After about five shots he caught the spirit of hitting hard. I saw he was not sideways to the net but stood almost facing it as he hit.

At the beginning he was erratic and missing. But then his shots started going in. Following one of his better shots he proclaimed, "Gee, that felt good," and he was on track, hitting with authority and accuracy.

Learning to Hit Unconventionally

For Don, following the conventional rule of getting sideways did not work. For Don and many others, facing the net is the way to generate power. The conventional closed stance, however, *does* work for some people. What's best for you is something that only you can determine, by experimenting. If you want to give the face-forward approach a try, read on.

(Don't attempt to follow my instructions in a mechanical fashion. If you have trouble picturing the positions and moves in your mind, take a look at the accompanying illustrations. If you still don't get it, simply do what I had Don do: Forget about getting sideways to the net and swing away until your shots start going in and going in with power.)

Let's assume you're right-handed and you want to hit a forehand. You begin by facing the net. You want to place yourself so that the ball, if left alone, would travel past your right side. How far away should it be from your side? The most comfortable distance for you to swing at it.

On a normal groundstroke, as you move to intercept the ball your right foot steps a bit to the right. Simultaneously your shoulders turn fully to the right, which transfers weight to the right foot. (The left foot stays about where it was so a line drawn through your ankles would be more or less parallel to the net.) The full turn of the shoulders forces your hips to turn. At the full backswing, your shoulders are facing the sideline while both feet remain pointing almost toward the net.

Closed and open stances. The top sequence shows
the closed stance. Feet, hips and shoulders begin sideways to the
net. The planted feet require reaching too far for the ball. In the

lower open stance the shoulders first turn while the feet face the net. At impact, the left foot has just stepped forward to attack the ball, with the body uncoiling powerfully.

As you swing, the left foot sweeps forward toward the net and comes down to catch your shifting body weight.

A Footnote on Backhands

Backhands pretty much work the same way, though of course on the opposite side. Step to your left with your left foot and twist your shoulders all the way to the left. Launch the swing forward off the left foot, landing on your right foot as you complete the swing.

Backhands *are* different in one respect. You may find that the open stance is more natural with two-handed backhands than it is with one-handed backhands. Standing in the traditional way with your side to the net may seem more natural and you may want to use it if you employ a one-handed backhand. Bradlee argued for facing the net in all cases. You need to find out what works for you.

The Source of the Power

What's the explanation for the added power that comes from facing forward?

When you turn your shoulders, your torso acts like a coiled spring. Power comes from the uncoiling along with the step forward. But something else is also happening and it involves one of the basics of a good tennis stroke—hitting through the ball.

With the open stance you are only halfway through the swing at impact. At the instant the ball is hit, your shoulders and hips are in line and the shoulders can still swing considerably further through the ball. In the closed stance, on the other hand, the swing is at least three-quarters completed at ball impact with much less power left for hitting. You can see this effect in the accompanying photo sequence.

The shoulder rotation is like a pendulum. You wind up on

the backswing, and you unwind as you swing through the ball. Your shoulders will be swinging their fastest at the center of their arc—right in front of your torso—just like the clock pendulum is moving fastest when it's halfway through its swing.

Some Unexpected Benefits of the Open Stance

You will react faster. As a result, you'll be able to stand closer to the net on your return of serve, which means you can get the ball back to your opponent sooner. And that puts pressure on him.

You will be more deceptive. Hitting with an open stance makes it difficult for your opponent to anticipate where you will hit. You can hit equally well to the right or left, something which is not as easy with the closed stance. When you turn sideways, the direction in which you line up fairly well determines where you will hit. Line up sideways for a down-the-line shot, and it's difficult to hit crosscourt safely. Why give your opponent the advantage of knowing where you'll hit?

Power Serving

It is not beyond the realm of possibility to increase measurably the power in your serve and to achieve this breakthrough in a relatively short time.

In learning to serve, you are taught the importance of snapping the wrist as you meet the ball with the racket. If you explore serving you will discover that the wrist snap is only part of the serve. Power should also come from at least two other sources: an upward drive of the legs and a rotation of the shoulders.

To get the most out of your serve, you need to drive

upward with your legs, unwind your shoulders *and* snap your wrist, all in one smooth sequence.

It takes practice. And experimentation. No one is able to explain to you how to coordinate these body movements of the serve with the toss of the ball. You have to explore it for yourself. Only by exploring the feeling of simultaneously driving upward while unwinding and snapping your wrist through the ball will you achieve a breakthrough in your serve.

As you explore, you will tinker with different parts of the serve and make adjustments that are comfortable for you. For example, you may discover that you are snapping your wrist too soon and that you are better off holding the wrist as long as possible. Think instead of accelerating your arm through the ball.

Believe it or not, you can develop a powerful serve in one session. Refining it and making it part of your permanent repertoire will require further practice, but the essential breakthrough can come surprisingly quickly.

A final note on the serve: Improving it is something to do when practicing. When you are playing an important match, focus only on making your racket strings drive up through the ball.

15

Stroking With Underspin, a.k.a. Backspin

HITTING WITH TOPSPIN OR HITTING FLAT IS FINE FOR groundstrokes and is the way most of us do in fact hit. But there are other strokes besides groundstrokes in tennis and for many of those, hitting with underspin works best.

Underspin (some call it backspin while others call a variation of it a slice) can do one of two things to a moving ball, depending on how the user applies it. In one instance the ball drops with little bounce close to the net, making it difficult for a player in back court to reach it. In the other, it sails deep into your opponent's court, putting him on the defensive.

Because you're hitting underneath the ball, underspin means you'll clear the net more easily, hit more cleanly and register fewer mis-hits.

You can simplify your game, and reduce the distraction of deciding how to hit every ball, if you adopt underspin as your method of hitting certain strokes.

Many intermediate players come close to hitting underspin correctly but they don't get it quite right. And imperfect underspin is often worse than no underspin at all. How is underspin achieved? By slicing at the ball. But contrary to what it may look like, a correctly executed slice does *not* mean simply hitting down or chopping on the ball.

Start the swing with your racket slightly higher than normal and move downward in a smooth, slicing motion. Just before it meets the ball—and this is the critical point—the racket should actually be rising slightly. You want to finish the swing with your racket high, not low. (A drawing of the motion would look like the curve of a banana.) Swing through the ball fully; don't baby the shot. Let the swing flow freely. Pull the racket smoothly through the ball with your hand, "butt first" style, leading the racket face through the swing.

Underspin works best with the following strokes:

Approach shots. This is the most natural shot to use it on, and many players running toward the net apply underspin without realizing it. But too frequently they over-slice. When it works, the ball plops over the net and skids to the side for a put-away. But just as often the exaggerated slice doesn't work. You're better off hitting slightly upward through the ball with the racket face open. The ball will sail deep into your opponent's court, setting you up for an easy volley on his relatively weak return.

Drop shots. Most intermediates attempt them by chopping down severely on the ball. That's the wrong way to do it. Occasionally it produces a decent drop shot (misleading the user into thinking he's on the right track and that repeated tries will bring perfection) but hitting down on the ball this way usually sends it into the net. On the other hand, the smooth, banana-shaped swing lofts the ball over the net in a safe arc and drops the shot just over the net, where your opponent will be hard-pressed to reach it.

Volleys. Step in and block the ball (do not swing at it). End the block shot with the racket rising slightly. The ball will land deep into your opponent's court and give you time to move in anticipation of his return.

Half-volleys. These are defensive shots, forced on you when the ball lands unexpectedly at your feet. Underspin can get you out of the jam. Hitting so that your racket rises as it meets the half-volley will reduce the chance of error on your return and gives it depth, putting your opponent on the defensive.

Occasionally it's not a bad idea to hit your normal groundstroke with underspin. Because the ball will bounce differently from what he has come to expect, it will disrupt your opponent's timing.

Hitting with underspin carries one other benefit: Making sure that you are slightly lifting your racket forces you to concentrate on that critical point of impact. Thus few mis-hits occur on slice shots but it is essential that your racket be rising at impact.

16

The Joy of Practicing

IMPROVEMENT IN TENNIS, AS IN ANY OTHER SPORT, REQUIRES practice. The more you practice, the more you're going to improve, and the closer you're likely to come to mastering the game.

There's a catch, of course: Many players don't like to practice, don't even like hearing the word. Others would be willing to practice, but just don't have the time. Odds are you fall into one or both categories and probably are saying to yourself, "He's telling me I'll never make a 'breakthrough' in tennis unless I practice hours upon hours. Well, there goes my tennis future."

No, that isn't what I'm saying. You can achieve a breakthrough even though you don't have the time to practice or resist the idea of engaging in formal practice sessions. All it takes is some adjustment on your part.

If practicing bores you, or if your tennis time is so limited that you can't or won't devote some of it to practice, then simply practice as you play matches. A lot of people do exactly that. As they play they explore, observe and change their games. Winning during those moments isn't important. (More on this approach later.)

But let's say you're in a different category. You're determined to become a much better tennis player, and you're willing and able to put in two hours of practice for every hour of play.

Top athletes achieve mastery of their sport because they are dedicated to practicing, not in order to win but because they view it as an end in its own right. Practice is a way of life with them, something they enjoy doing.

If tennis means a lot to you and you're ready to make a full commitment to bettering your game, then practice itself will be rewarding, fun and even therapeutic.

Practice and its Many Forms

There are many ways to practice—on the court, on the backboard, in front of a mirror. Whichever one—or ones—you choose, you'll find that your tennis technique will improve steadily, so long as you practice the right things.

At Home, at Work, on the Street

Reacting to the ball, as I've made clear, is one of the most important concepts in tennis. It is also a part of tennis that you can practice off the court and without a racket.

The easiest way is by pretending to hit balls. I do that carrying my fold-up umbrella when I walk around town. I visualize a ball coming at me unexpectedly—hard, soft, with spin, or at my feet—and react to the imaginary ball with my umbrella. I try to swing so my wrist naturally stays fixed, meeting the ball well in front of my torso.

Yes, I get a few strange stares from passers-by. I've learned to disregard them.

This innocent little exercise is a surprisingly effective way of engraving react-to-the-ball into your muscle memory. You can also use such off-court routines to groove hitting out in front, stepping into the ball and swinging compactly.

Even the way you react to the unexpected can be sharpened through what might be called "imagination tennis." Visualize balls coming at you at different speeds and landing at different spots nearby while you react with your umbrella.

By the way, it doesn't have to be an umbrella; a rolled-up newspaper or even your hand will do. And if you're too bashful to engage in this kind of drill in public you can do it inside, in which case you can use a real racket and swing while you're doing something such as watching television.

On the Backboard

Many tennis courts have backboards near them, but if there's not one where you play, simply find a substitute such as the side of a school building in a school yard. I've hit in indoor car parks and volleyed off the side of a barn.

I like hitting on the backboard. The solid thunk-thunk-thunk of hitting the ball and observing how I hit is soothing. You may find it so too, and it can really help your timing.

When you practice groundstrokes on a backboard let the ball bounce twice. Hitting the ball after only one bounce leaves too little time between shots. The ball comes back from the backboard much sooner than it would from your opponent— it's only half as far away—and causes you to rush your swing unnaturally.

You can groove your strokes on the backboard because you hit about six times as many balls, per half-hour, as you hit on the court. You're not wasting time picking up balls.

As you hit these hundreds of balls, be aware of your position, your body movement, your backswing, and your racket motion. The backboard returns them predictably, so you should usually be in position as you hit each one.

With Videos and Mirrors

It's valuable to see yourself swing and play. One way is to utilize a full-length mirror, either at home or at a health club.

The mirror is useful when working on timing. You can see what a smooth swing looks like because you won't be watching the ball. Swing your hitting system until it feels smooth and effortless, and see how that looks in the mirror.

Until recently the opportunity to see yourself on film was pretty much limited to those fortunate enough to be able to afford filming of their play. The advent of the video recorder opened up the option to many more of us. All you need is a battery-operated video camera. Simply set the camera on a bench near the net, aim it toward your court at the widest aperture, and let it run as you hit.

Let it record groundstrokes, volleys and all your other strokes. For volleys the camera will have to be aimed more toward the net. Most video cameras now let you rewind the tape and view yourself instantly by playing the tape back through the viewing lens.

When you view the video you may see flaws so blatant that you will wonder how you could be unaware of them. Or you may observe for yourself mistakes that had been pointed out to you by an instructor. But most important, you'll see your swing, and discover what your timing and balance are like and where you can improve.

Fifteen minutes of videotaping about once a month is useful. Tape yourself when you are playing badly, and when you are in top form. Tape your pro and some other good players, and some who play badly too. Study these tapes to see the differences.

It is particularly useful to tape your serves. You might hit a couple of baskets of practice balls, and later watch the video to see if you can discover ways to improve your balance. See if you are using your legs to drive up through the serve as you hit and are focused on the ball at impact. Most people are surprised, sometimes even shocked, to see how different their service is from what they imagined.

Zeroing in on Specific Problem Areas

Simply getting out on the court with someone and hitting balls for an extended period is a form of practice. If you both hit away you're bound to touch almost every part of the game. But there are times when you should be focusing on particular aspects of your tennis. What follows are drills and other forms of practice aimed at specific problem areas.

Hitting on the Run

Most tennis players warm up and practice by hitting balls to the middle of the court. In a match, your opponent isn't so considerate. He'll try to run you back and forth by hitting all over the court. Why not practice the way you hit when you play—on the run? Hitting on the run is good for practicing balance and timing, as well as recovery from wide crosscourt shots.

Ask your practice partner to stand in one corner of his court. You hit all your balls to that corner while he returns first to your backhand and then to your forehand, alternating back and forth. Only one of you will be on the run this way and the ball will stay in play longer than if you both move.

Your partner's shots should be rather safe, deep shots that cause you to move back and forth easily, not hard-hit balls you can barely reach. Do this drill for five minutes, then reverse roles and let your partner practice while you catch your breath. You'll need to trade off because this drill is demanding—but effective.

Serve-and-volley

Practicing the serve-and-volley would seem difficult to arrange but there is a way. It's not complicated and it can even be fun. All you need are three people.

Two players take one side of the net, but only one plays at a time. They alternate serving singles points to the third player who only receives. The key part of the drill is that the server *must* serve and then rush the net for a volley after each serve. This is the element that provides the serve-and-volley practice. The player returning serve tries to win the point with a passing shot or lob.

The member of the serving team who is not serving picks up the stray balls from the previous points, thus cutting down on the delays. (It's best to use at least six balls for this exercise.) To inject a competitive interest into the exercise, and to establish an automatic time for rotation, score the play. A point won by the serving team means a point for the team; a point won by the player returning serve means a point for him. The first side to reach 11 points wins the game.

During a game, change the service court every six points. Play at least three games so that each of you has a chance to practice serve-and-volley. Going around twice should give you about an hour of solid practice. The next time your fourth doesn't show up for doubles try it instead of Canadian doubles.

Hitting "Sitters"

A variation of the serve-and-volley three-person drill can be used for practicing shots that require you to run in—those short returns that you attempt to put away. The serving team again takes turns serving but this time the server awaits the return shot in back court.

The player receiving serve hits a short, soft return. The server runs in to put the ball away. The person not hitting again retrieves balls. It's a telling drill. Hitting sitters is not easy.

Focusing—and Not Focusing

One way that may help you understand the importance of focusing on the impact of your racket on the ball is to devote practice time to purposely not concentrating on that key moment.

Occasionally hit while deliberately thinking of the court you're going to hit toward. Observe the results. Then hit while closely watching the ball the last two feet before you hit, focusing only on the impact. Again, observe the results.

Hitting Softly to Achieve Racket Control

Racket control is important. It allows you to change the pace of the ball you hit. You need it for drop shots. If you can hit both hard and soft shots your opponent will need to be aware not only of where you hit, but also of changes in pace. That makes his reactions more difficult.

An effective way to learn racket control is to practice hitting soft, deep shots. You'll find it's much more difficult than hitting the ball hard.

Try hitting as softly as you can while still getting the ball beyond the service line. If you can do that over and over, you've achieved a respectable degree of racket control.

As a variation, try hitting on a backboard while standing five or six paces—fifteen or twenty feet—from the backboard. Hit controlled shots and let them bounce once coming back to you. To do this you will need to learn to hit gently with your hitting hand well in front of you. If you hit too hard the ball will be upon you before you can get set for the next shot.

This is an excellent drill for developing a volley. The ball comes back quite soon because of where you are standing, and that means you need to keep your racket in front of you all the time. Any backswing beyond your hip will force you to swing too quickly and forcefully. You'll lose control of the ball after two or three such hits. The trick is to hit more and more gently, rather than harder and harder, and to use less and less backswing.

When you can hit the ball 50 or more times against a backboard this way, your volleying will improve. I've found this works for volleys when nothing else seems to. I think it's because this is a safe way to hit. Standing at the net while an instructor hits balls at you is disconcerting.

Don't expect this backboard drill to be easy. Intermediate players have more trouble with this than almost any other exercise. Some players can learn the drill in a few minutes but others need to work on it for a frustrating hour or so before it clicks in. Once learned, it will do magic for your game. You will begin to understand and feel the importance of racket control, and how to perfect it.

For Those Who Can't or Won't Practice

If actual practice sessions are not for you, either because you don't have the time or because you can't abide the notion, consider practicing while you play matches.

Practice Doesn't Always Make Perfect

A frequent complaint of serious players is that they reach plateaus and then stay there for long periods. It's no wonder.

Too often you have a preconceived notion of what's wrong with your tennis and go about making a change. Perhaps it's a change that someone suggested, like "get ready sooner." So you practice and practice getting ready sooner. But if that isn't the real cause of your problem, then working on it won't really help.

Practice in these circumstances merely grooves the way you play. If there is some basic problem like poor timing that is holding you back, then practice reinforces the poor timing. That results in a plateau.

If you're on a plateau, then you're stuck somewhere. You're not working on the right thing. You're grooving the wrong things.

When You're Better or at Least as Good

When you play someone clearly not as good as you are and you're not in a tournament or team match, it's not a bad time to practice. You can also utilize ordinary matches with someone who is at your level. However, doing so can lead to loss of the kind of concentration necessary for competitive play. Instead of concentrating only on the racket meeting the ball, your mind will be on different aspects of your game and the odds are you won't be playing up to par. So be prepared to accept losing.

While playing these practice matches, be aware of your timing and balance, your position at impact and what your mind is doing. Try to keep the ball in play longer so that practicing can be extended. Instead of deliberately winning points, hit the ball so your opponent can reach it easily and return it more often.

Experiment with varying the speed of your swing, or the amount of topspin you apply. Swing hard with topspin, and observe your timing and balance. Then swing smoothly and observe them again. Use these easy, friendly matches to be aware of your game under varying conditions. Be aware of what you concentrate on as you meet the ball, as you recover from hitting, and as your opponent hits. Pay attention to what your mind does as you serve. As always, you should be focused on your racket hitting through the ball, and *not* on where you want the serve to go.

When You're Getting Trounced

When you're playing a match and losing hopelessly—either to someone far better than you or to a peer who is having a much better day—you might as well do something useful. Call it a practice session and experiment with your game.

See if your groundstrokes seem late and rushed. If they are, it's probably because your strong opponent is hitting returns that are deeper and harder than you are used to. Notice what this kind of play does to your game. Try to observe how your timing seems hurried, how you are not able to swing fully with your body. Are you swinging from the elbow, even wristing the ball as you swing late?

Become aware of what lack of balance feels like. See if you are late getting to shots, and observe how that affects your balance. See if you are off-balance, particularly on wide shots. Observe yourself overrunning shots, thereby hitting off-balance again, or being caught flat-footed or off-balance and not ready to move.

Don't try to fix these problems, simply observe them. Understanding non-balance and non-timing will help you understand balance and timing. And you needn't limit your observations to your own game.

Watch a few one-sided matches at the courts you play. We all like to watch the good players but try focusing on the losing players, observing their timing and their balance as they play. Analyze how their game is affected. Often you can learn more by watching what a struggling player does wrong than by observing what a good player does right.

17

Confronting Nerves and Choking

CHOKING MEANS BEING SO NERVOUS YOU CAN'T HIT YOUR normal way. You tighten up, physically and mentally.

Sound familiar? It should, since virtually all of us choke at one time or another while playing tennis and most of us do it often. What most of us do not do when we choke is to admit it to ourselves. If we did, we would be able to limit the damage it does.

When You Choke, Acknowledge It

If you choke in tennis, acknowledge it. Until you do, it will control you. Once you do, you'll find that you can live—and play tennis—with choking. You'll also find that you choke less and less.

Acknowledging that you are choking doesn't mean that you give in to it. Acknowledging that you choke is the first step toward breaking its hold on you. You learn to play without it interfering with your game.

Fighting choking is a little like trying to shut out the thoughts that sometimes keep you awake in the middle of the night. The more you fight these thoughts, or think about how much you want to go to sleep, the longer you stay awake.

Similarly, you may not be able to control the counterproductive thoughts that overtake you on the court, thoughts that cause nervous, tentative tennis. These thoughts are influenced by your experiences, heredity, physiology, environment, role in life and culture—not something you can change.

You may attempt to banish nervousness through sheer willpower: "I'm not going to choke." It's a hopeless effort, one that actually reinforces the problem.

Another reaction to choking is telling yourself, "Oh, here I go again, I'm choking. I'm going to blow it." And you usually do.

Instead of fighting or giving in to it, simply stop making such a big deal over choking. Don't fight it. Don't let it intimidate you. Accept the fact that nervousness may be creeping into your mind, just as fatigue may be settling in your muscles. You can't do much about controlling it so you might as well get on with the things you *can* control—like the action of hitting the ball.

Yes, you'll still miss shots but not nearly as many as you would otherwise. Your mind, instead of being obsessed with the notion of nervousness, will be able to focus on what it should.

Choking, and the thoughts that contribute to it, exert power over you only if you attach importance to choking. Stop attaching meaning to choking, allow yourself to choke and don't be surprised if choking loosens its grip on you.

18

How to Play When You're Hurt or Tired or Old

CONVENTIONAL WISDOM HOLDS THAT TENNIS, LIKE MOST other sports, favors the young and strong. Like other shibboleths about the game, it's not necessarily true. It might be for the pros. It doesn't have to be for you. In fact, injuries, fatigue or age can work to your benefit.

Tennis and Tennis Injuries

Late in his career, when he was starting to experience the aches and pains of age, baseball great Ted Williams enjoyed a particularly good season at bat. He told a sportswriter that as strange as it sounded, a sore shoulder was helping him hit. The shoulder hurt when he missed the ball, Williams explained, so he focused more on meeting the ball.

Turning adversity into an advantage worked for Ted Williams. Depending on the circumstances, it might work for you as well.

I'm not suggesting you compete when injured. Moreover, serious injuries require rest so they can heal. But not all injuries are traumatic. Most tennis injuries don't happen suddenly, but rather evolve from the way you play. They are usually caused by hitting improperly. Thus, you can utilize an injury to find out what's wrong with the way you hit.

The Author's Elbow

I achieved my breakthrough in tennis—and came to write this book—because I had developed tennis elbow. I'd lay off playing for a month and it would seem to go away; I'd start playing again and after a week it would come back.

I got rid of my tennis elbow when it prompted me to explore the way I hit. I temporarily gave up playing matches and focused on practicing hitting. For about two months I hit balls without playing a set. I came to recognize when my timing was right and when it was wrong.

I began my new regimen by practicing on a backboard, letting the ball bounce twice so I had lots of time to swing. I tried to hit so that my body and racket—but not my elbow— felt the impact of the racket meeting the ball. I wanted to spare my sore tendon any pain.

My elbow told me when I was hitting perfectly: It was when my elbow did not hurt. If I hit the slightest bit late, I'd feel it. I came to know with precision what late hitting was and knowing that made it easier for me to hit correctly.

During the two months that I explored the relationship between my elbow and hitting, my tennis improved more than at any other time before.

The Author's Shoulder

I had a similar experience later when I developed a sore shoulder from serving. I dealt with the problem by taking a basket of balls to an empty court and hitting serves. I put in many such practice sessions, observing how my shoulder responded to my swing. When I served well the movement in my shoulder was smooth and painless. When I served poorly my shoulder usually felt the stroke. I came to realize that what was taking place had a lot to do with both timing and balance.

With the tennis elbow, it was clear to me that hitting out front with perfect timing was important. With the shoulder nothing specific resulted. But my serve became more fluid and much more powerful. I surmised that avoiding a wrist snap made most of the difference, but the serve sequence was too complex to isolate anything clearly. I just served better and more smoothly as I focused on swinging so my shoulder did not feel any pain.

A Word of Caution

Notwithstanding what I've just said, be sensible. Don't automatically go out and hit while you're injured. My two injuries were the type that allowed me to experiment as I did. Yours may not be of that type and to follow my example might just aggravate your injury. Give some thought to it. If you think your problem can put up with some experimentation and you feel you could learn from the process, give it a try. Don't attempt to play through pain. As with other parts of tennis, only you can tell what is right. If you can't hit without pain, *stop* hitting.

Check with your doctor first. But see if you can find a doctor who plays tennis or at least understands how tough it is for a tennis player to take a rest from the game.

When Fatigue Sets In

Usually your muscles tire toward the end of a match. As they do, your timing changes and your reactions slow. If you've been using the same can for a while, the balls become soft, making it more difficult to put zip into your shots.

You don't play the same when you're tired and the balls are old. You don't play as naturally. But there are ways to compensate for your fatigue.

When your opponent hits, for example, make a conscious effort to keep your racket and hands up high, in front of your chest. When you are tired you have a tendency to let your arms drop. This slows your reactions since you must take the time to move your arms and racket upward before you hit.

When your legs tire, your swing weakens because you're not fully utilizing this critical part of the hitting system. More balls go into the net when your legs are tired. Compensate for the loss of power by hitting the ball with more loft to make sure that it clears the net and lands deeper in the court.

To reduce errors further, hit your returns to the center of your opponent's court. Going for the lines anytime is risky business; doing so late in a match is foolhardy and causes errors because your timing isn't sharp enough to support the accuracy needed.

Of course, the most important thing to do when you're tired is to focus even more than usual on reacting to and hitting the ball. When you're mentally weary, you really need to concentrate. Focus your thoughts on making the racket hit through the ball.

Keep in mind that your opponent is probably weary too. That's the time to grab the initiative by concentrating particularly well. Sacrifice hitting hard for not mis-hitting. Your opponent will miss more often. Don't do the same. Remember, every time you miss the ball you need to win the next two points to get back where you could have been.

Again, a Word of Caution

I've been talking about normal fatigue, the tiredness that comes over healthy and fit people who have undergone a hard workout. There are times when fatigue signals something else, something that might even be dangerous. Only you can make that judgment. My advice: If you have any doubts, stop playing.

Why Those Older Folks Win

Even though they don't run as fast or as often, older tennis players are forever amazing their younger opponents with their seemingly uncanny ability to be where the ball has landed and in position to hit it. The explanation is simple: They react early, hit deep, and anticipate well.

Years of experience have made these players aware of where you may hit most often in different situations. Consequently, they often start their moves early.

Since they hit deeply, they also have more time to react to your ball. The ball takes longer to be returned since you are deep in your court as you hit.

But even when they don't know where you will hit, they still react early. They begin to move before you hit. At this point it doesn't have to be in any particular direction; that can wait until they see where your ball is headed. But since they move more slowly they know they need to start moving sooner. They *react* well. They save half a second or more over someone who waits for their opponent to hit before reacting. A half-second may not sound like much, but tennis is a game in which seconds and fractions of seconds can make the difference between winning and losing points.

Tactics for Seniors

As you age and continue to play tennis, you will want to run less (so you save breath) and to make fewer quick moves (so you lessen the chance of injury). There are actions you can take to achieve both goals.

To cut down on the need for quick moves, hit deep shots to your opponent. That will give you more time to react to his return and make him run more. To hit deeply you will have to hit cleanly and consistently hit the sweetspot on the racket.

That in turn requires concentration, and here is where age can be an advantage: Concentration can improve with advancing years, rather than decline as physical skills do.

In order to run less, especially if you're playing a younger player, try hitting to the middle of his court rather than to the sidelines. Going for the sidelines is likely to mean more running for you since the balls returned to you from the sidelines will usually be severe crosscourt or down-the-line shots, both of which will require a good deal of movement on your part.

Your advantage over a younger player will be in steadiness, not in athletic skills. If you hit down the middle, your opponent will be forced to hit balls nearer the middle of the court. You will hit more balls, and your opponent may well miss before you do. Of course, if the opportunity arises for you to fire a ball across court or down the line, take advantage of it. But save your hard shots for those put-aways so they can't be returned.

Besides hitting to the middle, make your shots deep and soft. Young players become impatient rapidly, and will make errors trying to hit hard shots off your soft, deep balls. Younger players tend to practice with other hard-hitting young players and are used to hard-hit balls. Your softer shots disrupt their timing. I don't prescribe "dink" shots when I say soft. I mean the kind of shots that are hit with your racket coming up from slightly under the ball without topspin. Go for a natural deep trajectory to keep the opponent moving, rather than a series of lobs.

If you have been hit a short ball, move in with the intention of hitting a winner. That means hit deep and firmly. You want to make sure the ball is not returned. If it is, avoid getting into a running match. Just let the ball go. Don't even think about running back for a lob after you've come in. Say "nice shot" and be happy that you can live to fight another day.

Drop shots are particularly useful for aging players. They can eventually wear down younger opponents. A drop shot followed by a lob can tire your opponent fast. The other advantage of having a good drop shot—one that is well-concealed— is that the opponent must always be prepared for the drop shot, and that can disrupt the rest of his game. Most young players don't have a drop shot. It doesn't fit in with their self-image of hard hitting.

Walk Slowly and Carry a Big Racket

Between points and games give yourself time to catch your breath. Move leisurely as you retrieve balls and return to service court. This may frustrate a younger player somewhat, but as long as you don't delay the game unnecessarily there's no reason why you have to play at his pace.

Between games stop for a breather. Be sure there is a chair available to rest on. If not, bring a small folding chair with you.

As you age you will benefit from a larger, more powerful racket. Oversize and super oversize rackets provide more power. String them less tightly. Pancho Gonzales, now in his 60's, once yelled "37 pounds" to a spectator who asked him what his oversize was strung at. The usual tension is between 60 and 70 pounds. The larger, less tightly-strung rackets sacrifice some control, but as you age, you will compensate with more control in your game.

A Closing Word

Just because you're entering those advanced years don't give up on achieving breakthroughs. I expect to play better at 60 than I do now. There's no reason you can't continue to improve.

Like your tennis game, *Breakthrough Tennis* can only evolve and improve with further exploration. Your suggestions, insights and questions are welcome and encouraged. They may be addressed to the author at Box 387, Newington, Virginia 22122.

Rolf Clark, Ph.D., teaches "systems thinking," the study of mental and physical processes, at George Washington University in Washington, D.C. Beginning at age 41, he struggled with tennis for several years before devising his own way of learning the game. He rapidly became a ranked Seniors player and then a Certified Teaching Professional.

Dr. Clark is a graduate of Phillips Exeter Academy, Yale University and the University of Massachusetts. He currently lives in Virginia.

INDEX

For Additional Copies of

BREAKTHROUGH TENNIS

Write: Farragut Publishing Company
2033 M Street N.W.
Washington, D.C. 20036

Send me _____ copies at $9.95 per copy plus shipping charge of $1.55 per copy

Name _____

Address _____

City _____ *State* _____ *Zip* _____

Make check or money order payable to Farragut Publishing Company

For Additional Copies of

BREAKTHROUGH TENNIS

Write: Farragut Publishing Company
2033 M Street N.W.
Washington, D.C. 20036

Send me _____ copies at $9.95 per copy plus shipping charge of $1.55 per copy

Name _____

Address _____

City _____ *State* _____ *Zip* _____

Make check or money order payable to Farragut Publishing Company

For Additional Copies of

BREAKTHROUGH TENNIS

Write: Farragut Publishing Company
2033 M Street N.W.
Washington, D.C. 20036

Send me _____ copies at $9.95 per copy plus shipping charge of $1.55 per copy

Name _____

Address _____

City _____ *State* _____ *Zip* _____

Make check or money order payable to Farragut Publishing Company